THE LITTLE MAN

based upon a true story...

by

Abbas Kazerooni

Tate Publishing. LLC

THE LITTLE MAN Based upon a true story . . .
by Abbas Kazerooni

Published in the United States of America
by Tate Publishing, LLC
127 East Trade Center Terrace
Mustang, okay 73064
(888) 361–9473

ISBN: 1–5988614–5-X

THIS BOOK IS DEDICATED TO THE
LOVING MEMORY OF MY MOTHER,
MARZIEH KAZEROONI.

To Mehrbod,

I hope you have a
great Birthday mate.

All the best,

[signature]

11-18-05.

ACKNOWLEDGMENTS

I would like to thank my adopted family for sticking with me and helping me through what were dark days. I would also like to thank Shawn for making this book a reality.

CHAPTER 1

It was a typically hot day in Tehran as I finished my homework in my somewhat spacious bedroom. It was almost too big, but with very few contents. I just had my small bed in one corner, next to the radiator. I loved it there for the winters, where I could squeeze my toes in between the rails. Above my bed was a huge window, which looked out onto our back garden, if you could call it that. It was more like a garden attached to an orchard. I loved looking out of it on hot summer days when the sun was too strong to play outside. In the opposite corner was my little desk with its matching stool. Thinking back on it, I know that it was only a cheap little thing. It had a top that flipped open and shut, enabling me to keep my books inside. The best part of it was a secret draw where I kept all my little treasures. I wasn't really into toys; I preferred playing football and trying to make extra pocket money by any means possible. Even if I did like toys, I think I would have been disappointed, as it was wartime and my parents were not amazingly rich.

Our financial status was highly ironic as I lived in what was once a mansion. However, the lavish furnishings that I was told once existed were no longer there. In my huge room, I have already listed all its contents, apart from my plastic 100 Ryal football. I liked an empty room—to my mother's agitation, I would play football against the bare wall. It created hours of amusement for me.

My father used to tell me of the days how he used to be one of the richest men in Iran and how he used to mingle with royalty. That was until the Ayatollahs came in 1979 and took it all away. I could imagine it though, as I had seen all the pictures of our house with all the antiques, the paintings, and the gold that once decorated it. Our family was so famous that producers even made a 24-part series about us. My great-grandfather had started the Kazerooni dynasty. He was a self-made millionaire and had a monopoly on nearly all the businesses in the south of Iran. When the British invaded Persia, the government would not fight them, but my great-grandfather funded guerrillas to put up an opposition to them.

By the time my father was in charge of the family, we were mingling with royalty and government officials on a regular basis. This was of great importance to me, as it was the thing I boasted most about at school. If one knows anything about Persian societies, then they would know that the art of boasting is drummed into you from a very early age, not that I really needed any drumming. I never had or experienced any of this luxurious past, but that never stopped me from strutting around thinking that I did.

This day, however, was very different to all the others. I felt it from the moment I came back from school. I walked through the huge, black wooden door to my grandmother's delight. In her usual manner, she pinched my face to my disgust and planted two wet kisses on both cheeks with the usual, "I'm so happy you're home, my darling. Are you hungry?"

Usually, I would have answered with something like, "No thank you, Mamanjoon. I have to do my homework."

Even though I was a little monkey, I was, by my own recognition, a closet geek. I always had to do my homework before I could relax or eat. However, on this particular day, I had big problems. I had once again dominated the playground at lunchtime with my footballing prowess and torn the knee section of my trousers. The number of trousers my poor mother had repaired through my antics was beyond me. I knew I was in trouble, and it was on my entry that I decided to consult my biggest ally, Mamanjoon. As she opened the door in our usual routine, I sulked with my big, brown puppy dog eyes and had my head down. When Mamanjoon asked what the matter was, I merely looked at my knees and pointed to the trousers.

To this she merely replied, "It's okay, my darling. Go and take them off, and I'll mend them for you. It'll be our little secret."

Like a ferret, I was off to my room trying to dodge any attention coming from my mum or my dad. As I ran across the spacious living room floor, I noticed my parents were in heavy discussion on the lonesome sofa opposite our television. Their failure to acknowledge me was a sign that something serious was being discussed, but at this point, the situation suited my purposes.

So there I was in my room with nothing to do. I had finished my homework, and I couldn't play football in my room as both my parents were next door in the lounge. I sat there on my knees looking out of the window to begin with, but that was not satisfying my overly exuberant and energetic body. Therefore, I decided to find out what all the fuss was about. There was a long hallway that connected all the bedrooms and the family bathroom to the lounge. I lay there as quietly as I could, peering my cheeky, little head round the corner so that I could see what was going on. The lounge was as empty as my room. In the distant corner was an old white sofa facing a television, which was standing on a stall. In front of the sofa lay a colorful rug and a tiny coffee table. Above the television, there were still three family portraits of my father, my grandfather, and my great-grandfather. The rest of the walls were bare with stains of old paintings that once used to hang there. Most of the surfaces were collecting dust, as they lay bare. Only a few baby pictures of me lay about on the odd shelf, the rest was barren space. There were no objects between my parents and me. I had to be careful, as I could easily have been caught. My father's face looked worried and desperate. If there was something that I had learned about my father over the years, it was that he was neither of the above.

He leaned toward my mother, desperately trying to get his point of view across. "You know they won't give me a passport, don't you?"

This was obviously a rhetorical question, as even I knew that my father's passport had been confiscated at the turn of the decade by the new regime. He had told me that the Ayatollahs didn't want him to leave the country. I used to love it when he told me things like that. Afterwards, he always made me promise not to mention any of it in public, as it was really dangerous for the family. It made me feel like a man. My father had trusted me with this vital information.

My mother looked at my father inquisitively and questioningly replied, "Yes."

"Well, you have to leave with Abbas," was the immediate reply. As soon as this was mentioned, my ears were on full alert. What was he talking about? Where were we going? Passport? Are we going abroad? At first, I was excited, as it was a thing my friends and I used to boast about—who would go abroad first. Only rich, posh people ever traveled outside of Iran, and I was delighted that I might beat my friends to it. I remember seeing my mother's reaction. It was certainly not the same thing as I was feeling. I couldn't decide if she was sad or angry or possibly even both; I just knew it didn't look good. I was always closer to my mother, and seeing her like that immediately changed my mood. I just remember the light coming in from the window and shining off her smooth red hair. Her eyes were swelling up, and I wanted to be near her. I hated seeing her like that. It felt like Dad was pushing her a little. My father was a short man and much older than my mother. His hair was receding, and he had a beard. He always seemed to be calm, and yet he seemed to carry such authority with him. My mother, however, lost her temper much more quickly and yet always seemed so vulnerable.

All that Mum could say was "What are you talking about?" It was clearly above her comprehension. I certainly didn't understand.

"We have to get Abbas out of the country, my darling," he said with his deep, resonant voice.

"He's seven, for God's sake," she whimpered back, "just seven."

"That's exactly why we have to get him out now."

"How will he cope? He too young to understand . . . he needs stability, Karim." She was pleading with him.

Too young? I thought, *Just you try me.* My father stopped to look at her. Even he couldn't bear her tears. It must have melted his heart seeing her like that.

He wiped away her tears with his checked shirtsleeve and continued gently, "They've reduced the recruitment age to eight, Marzieh," he gently went on. "You saw Meenoo yourself the other day. Her son was brought back in a coffin, and for what? How old was he, thirteen?"

"Twelve."

"Well, there you go. You're arguing my point for me."

I couldn't believe what he'd just said. Recruitment was a popular topic of conversation, and I knew lots of children being signed up. At school, we were told that we would go to paradise if we died in the war. My father always begged me not to listen to them, and so I didn't. I knew better than to make fun of the children that went to war. My father had told me that it was a sad thing, but also stupid. If I'd repeated any of this, I would have been caned until I bled, and my father would have been whipped for sure, if not killed. But eight? I was eight in a matter of a few months. I always knew there would be a possibility that I might have to go to war, but never so soon. At that particular moment, I was frozen with fright. I didn't want to leave my mother, I was scared, and I certainly didn't want to die.

"Eight?" my mum suddenly said. "Are you sure?"

"Positive," he said sadly. "Bahman told me, and he gets it straight from the top." In my life, I had not really seen a lot of emotion from my father. I had seen him lose his temper only once, and that has stayed with me still to this day. However, this was the first time I had seen him get even a little sad.

My mother wanted to say something, but couldn't get it out. She could not come to grips with the concept of letting children fight at such a tender age. My father edged closer toward my mother. Then as he began to speak to her, he sensitively stroked her cheek with the back of his right hand as he so often did when he wanted to show her affection.

"They'll pick on people like us first, Marzieh. You know they will."

"But he's seven, for God's sake," as she broke down. She sobbed in my father's lap helplessly. Suddenly, Mamanjoon entered the room quite oblivious to what was going on. She was ninety-five, but extremely active for her age and very selective with her disabilities. She wobbled over nearer to the pair of them, with the aid of her walking stick. Her white hair covered her glasses as she crouched in her natural position.

She stared at my father as she said, "Tea anyone?"

"No thanks, Maman," he said horrified. "Maybe later." My father's disbelief was almost comical. Mamanjoon's timing was, as ever, nothing short of impeccable! Karim continued to stroke my mother's cheek while Mamanjoon was still standing there, looking at them like a lemon. I couldn't believe what I was seeing.

Karim then realized that his mother was still in the room when Mamanjoon spoke again, seemingly unaware, "Are you sure you won't have any tea? It's fresh!"

My mother raised her teary head with studied politeness as she spoke with her last ounce of patience. "No, thank you, Mamanjoon. Really, we're fine."

Mamanjoon sighed heavily, as if she'd been seriously offended and exited while hobbling dramatically. This little distraction had taken my parents' mind off the topic momentarily, and I could see the pain in their eyes as they looked at each other again. You didn't have to be a brain surgeon to see who would pick up the conversation again. I was as curious as anyone as I watched with my head in my hands, sprawled out in our hallway. I was watching my future unfold in front of me. I think I had not grasped what was really happening, but I kind of guessed and hoped that Mum would make it all okay. She always did. My father looked at my mother again with uncertain ease and spoke very quietly into her ear. "You have to go ahead with Abbas, and I'll make my own way . . ." He paused momentarily to gage a reaction, but continued when he didn't get one, "Somehow."

He was speaking quietly, and I was listening hard. I could hear everything. The lack of furniture made his voice echo like an ominous breeze. My mother looked at him with her moistened eyes.

"We can't leave without you," she murmered.

I wanted to run across the room and help her. I didn't know a life without my father. I knew nothing apart from the life that I had lived, and like any child, change scared the life out of me. Nevertheless, my father was relentless with his efforts. You could see he had made his mind up and really believed in what he was doing as he continued. "You have to go Marzieh; it's for Abbas' sake." I was a good twenty feet away when he muttered those words, but to this day, I know that I believed them. I was young and naïve, but I knew my father.

I think this was my mother's last real effort to stop this course of action as she wept into his lap. "But you are my husband and Abbas' father."

Even I had tears in my eyes now. I wish I had gone and given her a kiss. My belly was burning with pain; I was hurting because my mother was hurting. I am sure my father was in pain too, but I couldn't tell.

He retorted, as a matter of fact, "But Abbas has to come first. If that means we have to be separated for a while then so be it. You have to take him, Marzieh. You have to take him."

And that was that. My mother suddenly seemed to lose control, and she collapsed into his lap. I just remember my father holding her in his arms as he spoke gently into her ear to comfort her. I can't remember what he said; I just seem to remember his mouth moving up and down. I even got a glimpse of Mamanjoon standing in the kitchen doorway, wiping away her tears. I couldn't watch anymore. I went to my room and lay on my bed, and before I knew it, I had cried myself to sleep.

The next morning I automatically woke up before the alarm clock. I was facing the wall next to my bed as I opened my eyes. I knew it was too early for school, but something compelled me to turn round instead of closing my eyes again. As I turned my body over, I saw my father looking at me as he played with his worry beads. I squinted and rubbed my eyes. "Morning, Baba."

"Good morning," he muttered back adoringly. There was certain sadness in his voice. I knew something wasn't right; he had never looked at me like that before. Added to the argument with Mum the previous night, I knew there was something wrong. I sat up in my tight, little cotton pajamas and looked at him silently. He merely looked back at me in silence and carried on playing with his beads. I looked at the clock and then looked at Dad again as I questioned the situation. "What's wrong, Baba? It's 5 a.m. I have another hour before I have to go to school."

"I know," he replied. But that was it, he was not giving me the explanation that I expected, and so I looked harder at him. Then I got a good view of his eyes. They were blood red from crying and lack of sleep. There was more to it though. There was desperation in his eyes; he was looking for the right words. So I decided to make it easier for him.

"Are we leaving soon Baba?" A little smile crept to the side of his mouth as he stretched out his arms. Then with a knowing nod, he answered my question.

"When?" I asked inquisitively. I wanted to know what the reality of the situation was.

"As soon as possible, Abbas," he said profoundly, "as soon as possible." I didn't know what to say. I just sat on my bed and waited for him to continue.

I think he just decided to go in deep as he really took me by surprise with his next comment. "You're not going to school," he said abruptly. "You're staying home to help me and you mother."

"Why?"

"Because we have to prepare you for the trip. You could leave at any time." There was a slight pause as I tried to take in this information. Suddenly, my father's tone changed, and I felt like I was in a business meeting with him. He was talking to me like an adult. He knew me too

13

well; he knew that I would respond well to this, because I liked respon-sibility. I remember so well looking into my father's pensive eyes as he stroked his beard with his right hand and played with his worry beads with the other. I had never dreamt that maybe one day my father would be nervous while talking to me, and yet here he was in front of me.

After a brief pause, he tried to gather himself together as he said, "We'll tell the school you're ill. We'll tell them you're really ill and can-not attend any classes."

"But my friends will see me," I quickly retorted. There was a sudden pause. I knew his next sentence would not please me.

He uttered the dreaded words, "I'm sorry, Abbas, but you can't really leave the house again until the day we leave."

I couldn't quite grasp what he had just said. When I was not at school, I might have just as well lived outside. It was my only source of entertainment. I looked at him horrified. "What about my friends?"

"You can't see them again, Abbas. It's too dangerous." His voice wasn't so professional anymore. It had compassion in it now, as he knew what he was asking me to do. All my entertainment and joy came from playing outside with my friends.

I didn't know what to do, so I just asked the obvious. "Does that mean when we leave we won't say good-bye to them?"

"I'll say good-bye for you," he said. "If they find out we're tak-ing you out of school for any other reason than illness, they'll know we're up to something."

I considered his words carefully before I responded. "You're not coming with us, are you?" I suspected that he wasn't from his conversa-tion the previous evening, but I wanted to confirm it for myself.

"No," he said very simply. "I'm not."

"Is that because they took your passport?" I asked quietly.

"Yes," he responded. Then he paused as he tried to get his thoughts together. He was finding this very hard and so was I. I really wanted to cry, but I didn't because I was in front of my father. He stroked my wild hair as he spoke, "But I can't let them drag you into the army, Abbas. I won't let it happen."

"But I might not see you again," I said in annoyance.

"If you go to war, you definitely won't see me again." Those words silenced me momentarily. They really hit home with their simplicity, honesty, and reality. I could not imagine a world where I did not see him again. What he had said was beginning to make sense, but that did not mean that I was happy about it. There was a little pause as we both got our thoughts together. Then Dad was off again. This was by far the hardest thing I had ever had to cope with in my short life. It was probably one of the hardest things my father ever had to do, and he'd lived a long and distinguished life.

Unfortunately, there was more, as my father explained. "It's going to get hard in the next couple of weeks, Abbas."

"How do you mean?" I asked. "How much harder could this get?"

"Well, we have to sell a lot of things," he said, "things that are precious to us."

"Why?"

"Because we have to buy your tickets and get some money for when you get there," he replied.

Sitting still, I once again had paused the questioning so that I could come to terms with the information that I had been given. I knew the answer before he had told me. I was hoping that if I kept stalling the conversation I'd wake up; how I wished I were still asleep. I was lost as I looked out of my window to see the sun rising. I just remember my eyes welling up as I stared straight into the peachy orange sun on the horizon above our pine trees at the back of the garden. Thinking back, it must have been a beautiful morning, but it felt so ugly at the time. I was in my own little world as my father tapped me on the shoulder,

"Are you okay?" he asked in a concerned manner.

I turned round and nodded to show that I was. "Where are we going to go to Baba?" I asked.

"You and your mother will leave for Turkey, and there you will apply for a British visa. When you get it, you will go and stay with your cousin, Mehdi, who will help you until your mother finds her feet, and then you will wait for me there."

I was not sure what to believe, but at the time, honestly, I was more concerned with the logistics of the changes and the extent of them. I felt embarrassed for my father and myself as I asked the next the question.

"What are we going to have to sell, Baba?" I asked quietly. I was not sure how he was going to react and whether he was going to tell me the truth. He was completely taken back by the question though; I saw the surprise in his eyes. He kept calm though as he looked at me with a smile. I think he was quite impressed that I was thinking along those lines rather than thinking about my friends. I was very upset about my friends, but I knew that this course of action was really going to change our lifestyles but I didn't know how much.

My father laid a hand on my shoulder and stroked his beard as he spoke. "I'll be honest with you, Abbas," he said all grown up again. "Our lives will change dramatically in the next few weeks."

"How do you mean, Baba?"

"All the little luxuries that we take for granted will have to go," he said very seriously. "For example, the television will have to be sold."

"They only play religious stuff anyway," I said cheerfully. I could see that he appreciated my enthusiasm to help. I really was try-ing to make this easy for him, because his struggle to speak about the subject was blatant.

"All your mother's jewelry," he continued, "all of Mamanjoon's jewelry, the stove, pots, pans and . . ."

"And what, Baba?" I asked inquisitively.

"And your desk perhaps," he said, waiting for a reaction. He didn't get one though. I wasn't happy about it, but once again, I was doing it for the cause. I certainly wasn't as enthusiastic as I was about the television being sold, but there are limits to the patience of a seven-year-old sometimes.

He knew I was beginning to gradually lose my cool, and so he cleverly went on to justify it. "You'll need all the money we can get in Turkey," he said, as I quickly interrupted him.

"Turkey? Why are we going to Turkey?"

"You're going to Turkey because that's the only place you guys can go for now. From there you will try and get a visa for England, where your cousin Mehdi lives."

He was suddenly going too fast for me, and to his credit, he realized it quite quickly. He stopped speaking and looked at my gaze of confusion and asked, "What's wrong?"

"What a visa, Baba?" I asked quietly. I felt stupid, as I wasn't sure if I should have known the answer the question. He was very good with me, thinking about it now, as his answer was simple, patient, and understandable.

"It's a permit that gives you permission to visit other countries, but I'll tell you more about visas another time," he answered slowly. "Money," he went on, "will be very short from now on, Abbas. We have to cut out on treats, on expensive foods, or anything that isn't necessary." All I could do was look at him as he talked. Perhaps he thought he wasn't making himself clear. "Do you understand me?" I just nodded back at him and waited for him to continue.

"You're going to need all the money you can get in Istanbul, Abbas, because you'll be looking after Mum for me. I won't be the head of the family anymore, you will." I usually loved to hear that I am the head of the family and the man of the house, but this time round it didn't feel as good as tears rolled down my cheeks. Dad saw this as he stroked me on my head. "You can do that for me can't you, Buddy?"

I just nodded my head because if I had spoken I think I would have become hysteric. Dad could tell how vulnerable I was, and he let me calm down in my own time as he continued to stroke my hair lovingly. Eventually, I got hold of my emotions and took a long breath as my father had previously taught me and then just asked, "If I'm not allowed to leave the house, Baba, then what will I do during the day?" It was a fair question and he had a fair reply.

"There will be things that you and your mother will need to know about Istanbul. I will be trying to teach you as much as I can."

I just looked at him, and in all my arrogance, I asked him, "And how do you know, Baba?"

I had never questioned my father like this before, and he was as surprised as I was. I think he thought about shouting at me, but I had asked a good question in a situation that could excuse my insubordination.

He merely replied, "I have friends everywhere." That I couldn't argue with. I had seen more than my fair share of evidence that backed this theory up. People all over Iran knew of my father. I traveled with him on several trips, and I don't exaggerate when I say that sometimes people worshipped him. This was especially true in the south of Iran, as it was where he employed thousands of people at one time. Thus his last comment had put me back in my place. He could see I was going red, and since I'd helped him with his morning task he also helped me by moving the conversation on.

"When we're not talking about life in Istanbul, you can help me pack things so that I can go out and sell them." That brought a smile to my face because once again he had asked for my help. I had only dreamt of a day when my father would ask for my help. He could see my satisfaction and knew that it was good place to bring the conversation to an end. He was tired, and I had taken in far too much to digest in one sitting.

"Come on, Abbas, get back in bed. Go back to sleep. You can sleep in late today."

"And tomorrow!" I replied cheekily.

"We'll see!" he said with a smile as he tucked me in. He kissed me on the forehead and left the room. As he left, I could see that he was leaving a much happier man. He definitely got something off his chest, and it pleased me that I helped him do that.

I am not sure why Dad was telling me all this at such a time in the morning. There are many questions about my father that I am unsure of, and this is one. I have always wondered if he wanted to speak to me at this time so that he could talk to me about the trip before my mother could. This would have meant that he could have put it in his words rather than Mum's. I just hope it wasn't. Either way, his execution of the talk came as close to perfect as he knew how; I would respond to the concept of being a grown up and handling responsibility. I certainly took his bait.

CHAPTER 2

I woke up later on the same morning that I had spoken to my father. I strolled into the kitchen to get some breakfast when I saw my mother alone at the table. The kitchen was again very big with very few implements in it. The small wooden table and the four chairs around it dominated the space. Mum was sitting in her usual spot as I entered. She had definitely been crying, and as soon as she saw me, she wiped her eyes and smiled at me.

I didn't want to say anything, so I smiled back and greeted her. "Good morning, Maman."

"Morning, Darling. Would you like some breakfast?"

I nodded quietly to confirm that I did. She got up and went to the small white fridge next to the doorway. She got out the bread and cheese and put them on table. She was in her own world as I watched her move in automatic pilot. She then walked over to the stove and poured me a glass of tea and then came and sat down next to me. It was not unusual for her to watch me eat, but this was different. She knew that I had spoken to my father and was worried about me. At the same time, all I could think about was whether she was okay. I stroked the white cheese across the thin white bread while I thought about what to say.

Eventually, I built up the guts to say, "Are you okay, Maman?"

She reached out and held my hand lovingly as she spoke. "Yes, my darling," she whispered, "I'm fine."

I took a bite and started chewing slowly while watching my mother. She was watching me half with admiration and half with sadness. I think she was also trying to build up the courage to talk about what was going to happen.

"Are you okay?" she asked. I used my food as an excuse not to speak. So I ostentatiously chewed and shook my head to show that I was fine. She knew me better though. "Are you sure? You can tell me."

There was no way I could dodge talking about it now, so I decided to be brave about it and took the conversation head on . . . again. "No, I'm fine," I said.

"It's okay to have your doubts, you know?" she retorted. I knew that she was scared, so I felt safe to show my concern. However, I didn't want Dad to hear any of what I was going to say, because I was scared that he would think less of me.

I looked over my shoulder carefully, and then I muttered, "Where's Dad?"

Suddenly, Mum realized why I had been hesitating to talk to her. She was extremely understanding about it. She smiled at me, stroked my hair, and whispered, "It's okay. Dad's gone out to see if he can get the tickets. Mamanjoon is in her room listening to her radio."

I smiled, as Mum was the only person that really understood me and showed great sensitivity to my biggest insecurities. That is why she was the person that I was closest to, and I respected her by telling her how I really felt.

"I'm scared, Maman," I said. "I don't to want to leave without Baba." Maman raised her eyebrows as if to say that she felt exactly the same way. She knew, however, that she could not agree completely, because it would have undermined the conversation that I had with my father earlier that morning. Therefore, she tried to play it diplomatically.

"I know my darling. I feel the same, but Baba is doing this because he loves you." She paused to see if I was going to cut in, but I didn't. So she continued, "It's not good for him either, you know. He'll really miss us, and he'll feel lonely. He's only doing this because he thinks it's the best thing to do."

"And is it?" I asked. I did not want to cry again, and I had also promised my father that I would be strong for my mother. I could see that Mum was having difficulty in answering the next question. To this day, I believe that her answer was a lie and not in fact what she really believed.

She looked at me as sternly as she could and said, "Yes. It is the best thing—for you, Abbas." She knew she was lying to protect me, and I also knew it, but I decided not to dwell on the topic. Mum felt the tension, and so she carried on with what she felt like she had to tell me.

"It'll be really hard for us now, Abbas. None of us will like what is about to happen, but we have to be there for Baba like he is being here for us."

I suddenly thought that she had changed her mind and was telling the truth. Her attitude was completely different. She spoke with real coldness and was backing her husband completely. Even though I was taken back, it did make me feel better because it gave me more confidence in my father's actions.

"Now eat your breakfast, put your dishes in the sink, and go and have a shower."

"Do I have to have a shower?" I asked. I looked at her trying to persuade her by putting on my cute face. She'd seen it far too many times and wasn't buying it for one minute.

She turned round and looked at me with her motherly face and said, "No arguments. Have your shower, and then you're going to help me pack things for sale."

I did as I was told and finished my breakfast and went for a shower. When I came out of the shower and passed Mamanjoon's room on the way to my own, I saw the silhouette of my mother lingering over Mamanjoon's bed. I was dripping wet but curiosity got the better of me. I decided to see why my mother was there as she very rarely ventured into Mamanjoon's room unless she was ill. I put my face to the crack of the old, shabby door to see inside. My mother was obviously distressed at something as she sat on the bed next to Mamanjoon. Mamanjoon's radio crackled on a stool next to her bed. She lay there frail and somewhat disturbed. Mum leaned in over Mamanjoon, and her body gesture showed desperation.

My mother's tone was weak and childlike as she spoke. "Please, Maman. You have to speak to him. We can't just up and leave Iran like this."

I was really taken back. A few minutes ago, Maman was backing all of my father's plans, and here I was witnessing her trying to undo them. There was nothing shifting me now. I had to see the outcome of this conversation. If Mamanjoon allied herself with my mother, then they would have had a good chance of convincing my father to turn his decision.

"You have to go, my girl. There's no choice," Mamanjoon replied in a wise, soft tone as she held my mother's hand. I think she really did see the situation from Mum's point of view, but she also saw the bigger picture as did my father.

However, my mother had not gone in there without the intention of making a good attempt to win her vote. "But there is a choice. I choose to stay here with you and Karim. Abbas needs all his family."

Mamanjoon could see the strain on her daughter-in-law, but her tone and body language were suddenly not sympathetic. They were not aggressive, but showed authority and an old-fashioned wisdom that she sincerely believed in.

"I know things are different now, but we must still realize where we stand in the bigger picture," she said. My mother was not going to lose her emotions, but I could see her having to calm herself internally. Mamanjoon continued, "In my day, we married because were told to. It was our duty. I knew my place, Marzieh. Even if my husband was wrong, I still obeyed him."

My mother's response was cool, monotone, and clinical. She was not being rude, but she wanted Mamanjoon to understand her. "I wish I could be a strong as you. You have so much to believe in, but I don't have that feeling for the past." She stopped to take a breath but continued quickly in order to finish what she wanted to say. "I'm not sure I believe in anything anymore other than my son and my husband."

Mamanjoon took in what she'd just heard. She raised herself up from the bed and sat next to my mother. She then put her arms around her as she spoke the following words into her ear, "Then you must obey your husband and save your child. That is the least you can do." In her own opinion, Mamanjoon was being sensitive and yet truthful to her beliefs. I think she really believed in her son's actions and was behind him one hundred percent. I would have been interested to see if she would have reacted with the same old-fashioned virtues if she were losing her husband. My mother knew it was the end of the conversation and not worth pursuing. She had tried to do the thing that she thought was best for everyone. Once again, her plan had failed, but it did confirm the level of her sincerity with me earlier and her belief in a family unit. However, I knew not to question her about her loyalty to Dad's plans, because it would have started another argument between the two of them. I merely tried to deal with all the information I had heard and been given by myself. It didn't all make sense to me. It did mean, however, that I had to mature quicker than I expected. I am not sure I was aware that I was maturing, but I guess I was adapting to the situation that I had been thrown into instinctively.

A bit later, Dad ran through the door waving some papers about. He sat down next to Mum and me, around the wooden table in the kitchen. He was slightly out of breath, sweat was dripping from his forehead, and he was playing with his worry beads. Mum calmly got up, walked over to the fridge, and poured Dad a cold glass of water. She put it in front of him and sat down again. Dad downed the glass in one go, and then he began to talk. "It was almost impossible to get tickets to Istanbul," he said frantically. "All the airlines are fully booked."

"So what happened?" Mum asked, half hoping that we were not going anymore.

"I managed to get some, but the earliest tickets are only one week before Abbas' birthday," he said before pausing. I don't know what kind of reaction he expected, but he only received silence.

"I see," were the only words Mum could mutter after an ugly pause.

"But they were very expensive," he said sadly, "because everyone wants to go to Istanbul at the moment." I looked at him, not knowing what to do or say. He looked back at me and tapped me softly around the head like when we used to wrestle. Behind that tap was a lot of anxiety and stress. As hard as he tried to be strong and put up a front, I could sense all these feelings from the way he spoke and his body language. He used to play with worry beads to stop himself from biting his nails, but now he was using them like he really was worried. My father then turned to my mother who was staring blankly out of the window.

"We have to sell everything, and I mean everything," he said.

"Yeah, you said that before," Mum replied ambivalently.

"I had hoped we could spare a few things," Dad retorted sadly, "but the tickets set me back a small fortune."

There was a silence as we all looked at each other. Mamanjoon, like an old master, chose a perfect time to hobble into the kitchen. Not noticing the tension in the air, she came over to Dad and kissed him on the forehead. She then went over to the stove and then looked at us all.

"Tea anyone?"

I think mum was seeing the funny side to Mamanjoon's untimely interruptions as she merely replied, "Yes please. We'll all have a glass, thank you."

"We will?" Dad mumbled, being taken back by Mum's response. "Yeah, sure. Thanks, Maman."

I think Mum just wanted to keep Mamanjoon busy for a bit while we ended the conversation. If she were busy, then she wouldn't ask any questions or forget that she'd already asked us if we wanted tea. Then reality hit home again as we were discussing our financial situation. I was really worried for us, but I was excited too. I had never been involved in conversations like this before. Realistically, I was not a participant, more an observer, but even so, my inclusion kept me happy. I liked knowing what was going on.

Dad wiped his forehead and then said, "You guys need to have as many dollars as we can get our hands on."

"I can get a job," I said. I meant it too. I always wanted to make my own money. In fact, all my spare time had gone into how I was going to make more money than the week before. Realistically, however, I knew the response I was going to get and sure enough I got it, a mere stare from my father. However, he did go on to explain himself, and he was creative.

"No, Abbas. You can't be seen out, remember?"

"Oh, yeah," I replied, remembering the hard facts. Nevertheless, thinking back on it, my father was clever. He didn't use the real fact that I was too young to work as an excuse but rather a technicality, which in turn made me feel better about myself. Once again, he fooled me and even brought a little smile onto my mother's face. It had been a few days since I had seen it, and every time she did smile, she made us all smile. It was ever apparent that my mother did really love my father, because it was moments like this which made my mother smile or laugh. It wasn't an ordinary smile either. She had two sorts of smiles and laughs. She had a general smile, which most people saw. Then there was second kind of smile that she only brought out if Dad or I did something. It had a sincere love to it, and this was one of those occasions. This second smile was the contagious one. Whenever it made an appearance, without exception, her happiness made those around her happy.

I couldn't believe how fast things were moving. I thought that because I wasn't going to go to school, things would move more slowly, and I would be bored at home. However, I can't remember being fed up during the waiting period. The adrenaline and the preparation were a kind of an education anyway. I don't think I can express myself in a way that shows my gratitude for my father's thoroughness in preparation. He tried to foresee almost every scenario that might occur, and I have to say that he did a fantastic job.

The next morning I was in bed thinking that I was going to get to sleep in, when my mother woke me at the usual time as if I were going to school. She tapped me on my shoulder as I faced away from her. "Come on, Abbas. Time to get up."

"But I'm not going to school, remember?" I muttered in all my sleepy annoyance.

"Yes, but you still have to help me pack things up," she said smiling. "Don't think you can get away without doing anything you little monkey."

"Ahhh," I groaned. I turned round and looked at my mother as if she were punishing me unfairly. "Do I have to?"

"Yes, you do. Now get up and get washed," she said firmly. "We've got a long day ahead of us." There was no point in arguing, and I knew it. So up I got, stumbled into the bathroom, and took a shower.

After breakfast, I was summoned to my room to empty my desk and put all the contents into a cardboard box. Therefore, off I went into my room and opened up the lid of the desk. It was surprising what I had collected and forgotten about. The only thing I was aware of was my piggy bank, and I knew exactly how much was in it, but the rest of the contents were a slight mystery. As I looked through my things, it was like discovering them all over again. Pens that I had lost and suddenly found again, stones that I had picked up on my travels with my parents, things I had made myself, and even photographs of my family. It was a strange feeling, as I didn't want to empty my desk. The items that I was putting in my box were almost worthless to me the previous day, but suddenly now they seemed to be priceless. I also realized the reality of the situation; these were the only things that I possessed. It was a frightening and sad concept. I wasn't even sure what I was allowed to keep. Did they want my desk or my belongings? The only thing that I was going to fight for was my piggy bank, as it was the thing I treasured most. From a young age, I had learned to work for money, and that is where most of it had come from: cleaning windows, sweeping the patios and the garden, washing dishes, cutting hedges, and picking fruit. This was a value that my father had drummed into me from a very young age, and I liked the fact that he respected me when he gave me money.

After I had filled my box and my desk was empty, I filled another box with old clothes that were too small for me. I was never bothered about clothes, as I tended to rip most of them anyway, and that was not so difficult. When I finished, I strolled into my mother's room where she was doing exactly the same thing as I had just been doing. It was the first time I think I saw an expression that I could not only understand but share with my mother. Her face told me everything. She was going through all the feelings that I had been going through only a few minutes prior. Only she seemed more upset. It was because she was obviously removing so many more memories. She was putting away photos that I had never seen before. These were photos that had been taken at the turn of the revolution and hidden in cupboards.

I walked over to her and took a look over her shoulder. It was a picture of my father dancing with my mother in a tuxedo and she was wearing a chic, red ball gown. I couldn't believe it. The photo was like a Hollywood picture. She looked so beautiful, he looked so handsome, and they looked so happy. That moment alone showed more happiness than I had seen in my lifetime. You could see how much in love they were by the way they stared into each other's eyes. I could see the sadness on my mother's face as she looked at the picture. I put my hand on her shoulder.

I didn't know what to say, but I wanted to help her. "Are you okay, Maman?"

She just nodded. I could see that she was trying hard to keep it together for my sake.

"I know how you feel, Maman. I didn't want to put my things in the boxes either." I wasn't sure if that helped or not, as she didn't say anything, but I was sure she had registered what I had said.

"You know this picture?"

"Yeah," I replied inquisitively.

"Do you know where it was taken?"

I had a closer look and I couldn't figure it out. I just knew that it looked very grand, like something out of a film. So I put the photo down and shrugged my shoulders, suggesting that I was giving up. My mother smiled and pointed to the floor.

"What?" I said. I didn't quite understand.

"Here," she said softly, "it was taken here. We were dancing in our lounge."

"But it looks so different."

"We were different, my darling," she said as she brushed my hair with her hand. "We were rich. We were very rich." My mother was suddenly in a different world as she placed herself back in that night. She took so much delight in recounting the events of that evening. So she continued, "You know the windows to the patios?"

"Yeah."

"They were taken out so that the lounge spilled into the garden. We had a path that ran from the pool into the orchard and a marquee about thirty feet to the left of the pool. Can you imagine?" I just shook my head in disbelief. It was truly amazing, as I could not imagine it. "There was a band playing, and there were about three hundred people here that night."

"Three hundred?"

"Three hundred," she repeated with joy. "Some very important people were here, Abbas."

"Who?" I demanded.

"Darius . . ."

"What? The singer?" I shouted in all excitement.

"Yes, the singer," she giggled out. She seemed almost as excited as I was as she recreated the evening. Then she went on, "Persia's foreign minister, at the time, was here, and it was also the same night that your father proposed to me."

"Really?" I asked. I had forgotten everything else; I was so engaged with the story.

"Yes, he asked me in front of everyone. Then Darius sang to us while we danced in front of everyone."

"Wow," I groaned in disbelief.

"It was one of the best nights of my life. That was my life, and here these fools are, taking away what I have left." I could see tears rolling down her cheeks as she spoke. Without knowing it, I began to cry with my mother, but it was more than mere sadness. It was a feeling and understanding of my mother's pain that was the most unforgettable thing about that morning. It was a feeling and a moment that I shared with her. I had never before really known what I had missed in my life and what should have been mine until this day. Yet it must have been worse if you had it and then lost it, which is what happened to my parents. I didn't think of my father at the time, but now I know how hard it must have been for my father too. It was possibly harder for him as he took great pride in seeing himself as the provider of the family. He always did provide, and I was never really short of anything when I was with him, but I can only imagine that he must have lost face in front of my mother. I don't think that my mother saw it that way and neither do I, but I remember his mentality and the way he saw life. He always told me that ultimately only you could take responsibility for your own situation.

Over the next few weeks, my mother and I had brief lessons with my father where he told us the do's and don'ts of Istanbul. He had spoken to his friends who either lived there or traveled there a lot on business. These lessons were pretty informal, until only a few days before we were to leave. My mother and I were sat on the sofa in the living room. The room echoed with every noise, as everything had been sold or was waiting in boxes to be sold. My father was strolling up and down the room asking questions, and we would answer like a little quiz. He looked so worried. He was sweating heavily to the extent that his shirt looked completely wet. Sweat dripped from his head, and he was playing with his beads.

As he walked to the window, he stared out onto the main street and then said, "So then, what do you do for money when you get to Istanbul?"

"We only swap $20," my mother said patiently. She could see that he was stressed.

"Why only twenty?"

I answered in a way that showed I was bored and knew only too well, "Because we can get a better exchange rate on the black market."

"Don't get smart, Abbas," he snapped. "This is for your own good." I was shocked at his reaction and shut up quickly. My mother grabbed my arm to comfort me silently while my father carried on.

"So then, what do you when you've swapped your $20?" he asked with a softer voice. I think he could tell that he'd overreacted.

"We get a taxi and check out the hotels that your friend is going

to suggest, and we choose the best one for us," my mother profession-
ally replied. It was like a formal business meeting.

"Yeah, I'm calling my man in Istanbul tonight to get the names
of the hotels," he said sharply to show us that he on top of everything.
"Remember that these hotels will be where a lot of Iranians will hang
out. Be polite and courteous to them, but not too friendly. If they're
around, the locals won't try and rip you off, as it'll seem you know your
way round, and you know the rates." He paused to think what else he
could ask. Suddenly it came to him. "What should you try and avoid?"

"We should try and use the buses rather than taxis, as they're a
lot cheaper," I said quietly.

"Good. What else?"

"We should avoid going out at night," I said more confidently. I
think my mother was bored with this now as it was patronizing her but
she kept silent.

"And?"

"We shouldn't tell anyone how much money we have," I said
remembering that point.

"That's very good, Abbas."

"Thank you, Baba."

"Try not to eat out, as it's too expensive . . ."

" . . . and we don't know how long we're going to be there . . . I
know, Baba."

"Right," he said hesitantly. By this stage, he probably thought
that he was getting boring too. "Good lad."

"And Baba?"

"Yes?"

"We shouldn't ask for favors from anyone unless it is an emer-
gency, because they will expect a bigger favor in return," I said trying
to prove my knowledge.

"Good lad, you're learning fast." As he said that, he noticed a
blue van drive down our street and stop outside the house. "Ah, here
they are, the last of the boxes are going."

My father then went to the door and opened it to let in two strange
men. They were younger than my father, both with beards, wearing gray
suits with shirts and no ties. They followed my father into all the rooms
and looked at what they could take, and then proceeded to take anything

that they wanted. They kept coming in and out of all the rooms and took boxes, figures, paintings, pots, and pans until they reached us in the living room. The television had already gone. The only thing that remained was the sofa we were sitting on. Nobody had to say anything. My mother and I automatically got up. My mother held me and shepherded me to the other side of the room as the men took the sofa out into their van. I could see my mother was holding back her tears. I had never seen our family cry so much but it had all been behind closed doors. This time I could see that my mother would not cry, even if it killed her. She would not reduce herself to cry in front of a stranger.

My father then went outside to talk to them, and I went over to the window to see what was happening. They were obviously in heavy discussion about the money, and I could see my father trying to control his emotions too. He fought with all his might to get every Ryal that he could. Eventually, he gave in and they all walked back into the house. I could not see what else there was to sell to them. They went toward the direction of the bedrooms. Then they came out with my parents' bed. I could see my mother clinch her fist as she saw her own bed disappear. She could not bare it anymore, and she had to go into the garden. Then Mamanjoon's bed came out, which is what surprised me most. If anyone needed a bed, it was Mamanjoon. The men stayed outside this time. My father took the money and came inside only to be greeted by me. H e put his hand on my head and forced a false grin as he spoke,

"Mamanjoon's bed is more expensive than yours. I told her she can have yours."

"For sure, Baba. I like sleeping on the floor anyway. It's good for your back," I said enthusiastically trying to make him feel better.

"You're a good boy."

"Dad, come with me, will you?"

"I'm busy at the moment, Abbas. Can it wait?" he asked softly.

"It's important," I said, "it'll only take a few minutes." He nodded, and so I took him to the garden and through to the orchard. I then saw my tree and began to dig under it.

"What are you doing, Abbas?" he asked.

"Wait a sec, Baba," I said as I dug hard. Then I got to my plastic bag that I had hidden. In it were my piggy bank and three account books for my three savings accounts. I handed it to him, and without opening it I said, "The first account has 5600 Tomans in it, the savings has 11000 Tomans in it, the third had 4125 Tomans in it, and the piggy bank has 567 Tomans in it."

"Abbas, this is your money, I can't take . . ."

"I know it's mine, Baba, but I want to help."

He looked at me in the eyes, and he could tell that I really meant it, and then he grabbed me and hug me in a way that he had never done so before. I felt quite uncomfortable with it to be honest, as my father had never shown that much affection toward me. I always knew he loved me, but he was never the kissing and hugging type. He then kissed me on the head and said, "Thank you, Abbas."

CHAPTER 3

It had been a long month with almost all my patience being tested fully. I remember the day we were meant to leave. Dad was out changing the money into dollars, and the house was so quiet and empty. My father had left the changing of the money until the last moment in order to change all of it in one go. That way he would not be charged for the change more than once. My bag and my mother's bags had been packed the previous night, and they stood by the door waiting. I was changed and ready to go. I walked through all the corridors and the rooms, and it felt so empty and bare. Every little noise echoed as I walked around the house in search of my mother and Mamanjoon.

As I entered the kitchen, I saw the two of them sitting on the floor with a plate in front of them and some dried bread. My mother signaled for me to come and sit next to them. Mamanjoon smiled as she spoke to me.

"Come over here, my darling. You should eat before leaving," she murmured. "It's going to be a long day."

"What is it?" I asked. I didn't care because I was hungry, but it was making conversation. It was already apparent that everyone was trying to avoid the inevitable.

As I peered over the plate, my mother whispered, "It's only fried onions with bread, Abbas." She stopped to compose herself before continuing, "That's all we have left."

I couldn't have been more disgusted, but I was hungry, and I could see that my mother was upset. So I sat down and took the smallest portion I could and put the fried onions on a piece of dried bread. I opened my mouth only to see both my mother and Mamanjoon watching with great interest. After taking a small bite, I chewed very carefully expecting the worst. To my great surprise, it wasn't half bad. So I continued to chew and helped myself to another portion. I didn't know fried onions and bread could be that nice, but I had never had to eat just onions alone.

"I knew you would like it," my mother said.

"So did I!" I responded with a little arrogance. My pretence of not being scared to eat the food was not being bought, but it did amuse her though.

Whilst Mamanjoon was clearing the plates away, the door opened. It was my father. He had a fake smile on his face as he brushed his beard with his hand, and then reached for his worry beads.

"Time to go, guys," he said trying to be strong. "Say good-bye to Mamanjoon, Abbas."

I walked over to Mamanjoon and stood in front of her. In her traditional manner, she held my cheeks with both her hands and kissed me, "I'll miss you, my darling. You take good care of yourself and always remember that you are a Kazerooni. I've prayed for you, and I will continue to pray for you."

"Good-bye, Mamanjoon," I said as I began to sob. I had not expected to do this, but it just came out.

"Come on now, Abbas. Men don't cry. You know that," she said with a gentle smile. "You're a Kazerooni, remember?" She tidied my hair and her last words to me were, "Be strong, my boy, be strong."

I gently moved over to the door and waited for my mother to say good-bye to Mamanjoon. Mamanjoon walked straight up to my mother and hugged her tightly as she whispered in her ear, "You're doing the right thing, my girl."

"Good-bye, Maman," my mother replied with tears in her eyes. My father then threw me some keys that I didn't recognize.

"I've borrowed a car from a friend to take you to the airport," he said. "It's the black one outside the door. Put the bags in the car, Abbas."

I sat in the back of that car as my father pulled away slowly, trying to avoid the potholes in our street. I saw all the houses in our street pass by me for the last time. All my fondest and saddest memories flashed by me in that minute. All the times I had played football, all the times I had ripped my trousers or shoes, all the fights I had been in, all the mischief I had caused and the number of times my mother had come to find me along the street. I knew that the airport would be bad enough, and so I managed to stop myself from crying.

The car was moving quicker and quicker as we moved onto the main streets and eventually onto the motorway. No one had spoken since we had left. Both my mother and I were trying hard not to cry. I could see that my father was now really feeling the stress. He had his elbow out of the window and his head slightly tilted as he drove in automatic pilot. He was trying to cover all the angles and think of some last minute advice to give us. He was bothered but he was also desperate to try and keep calm. I could see his brain ticking and I knew that it was just a matter of time before he spoke. Suddenly, out of the blue, he came out with, "What's the capital city of Turkey, Abbas?"

I was taken back by his question. I didn't know if it was a trick question, or he was trying to keep the atmosphere light. So after a brief pause I muttered out, "Istanbul."

My father smiled and then looked at my mother. My mother turned around and looked at me with a smile. I sighed with relief as I thought I had got it right. Then my mother said, "It's Ankara, but it's a common mistake to make. A lot of people think it's Istanbul," she said, as she jokingly slapped my father on the shoulder. "He's just trying to trick you."

That little incident was enough to take our minds away from the reality, even if it was for a few minutes. That is all I remember from the journey. I cannot remember the roads, what I saw, or what was said apart from the above-mentioned conversation. I know, however, that I looked out of the window for the majority of the journey, hoping it would never end. It was a journey that seemed so long and arduous. The longer it went on, the more hope I had that we wouldn't go. However, the further we went, the more nervous and sad I felt, because I knew that the reality was that we were going no matter what.

Eventually, my father parked at Tehran Airport near the terminal. There was deadly silence in the car as we all prepared for the inevitable. I could hear my mother breathing deeply trying to control herself. My father was looking straight through the windscreen at the wall ahead of him with an emotionless face. However, I could hear him reaching for his worry beads inside his left trouser pocket. We were only stationary for about twenty seconds, but it felt like a lot longer than that. It was a family moment as well as an individual moment for us all. Suddenly, my father snapped us out of our reverie. "Come on, guys, we've got to get you checked in."

He opened the door to leave me sitting still and not moving. My mother noticed this on her way out of the car. She popped her head back in and with a gentle smile said, "Come on, my darling. It's time to go."

I got out of the car slowly and went round the back by the trunk where my parents were. My father got the two bags out of the car. He looked at us, took my bag, and started to walk. My mother tried to carry her own bag when I stopped her. "I'll take it Maman."

"But it's heavy, my darling," she said.

"I'll manage," I insisted.

She saw my determination and then began to walk along with my father. I hobbled behind them struggling with the heavy suitcase. My father went in through the main airport entrance where thousands of people were sitting, eating, talking, and queuing. My father stopped momentarily to have a look at a screen. He then turned round to my mother and asked, "What's the flight number again?"

"IR391," I cut in immediately.

My mother nodded to confirm. I could see that my perspicacity had put a smile on my father's face. All of a sudden, he had a spring in his step. He looked at the screen again and then began to lead us to a check-in desk about fifty yards away to the top right of the terminal. Once again, I struggled behind with the suitcase, but I also had been given a boost by my father's confidence in me. About twenty feet from the check-in desk, my father suddenly halted and waited for me to catch up. He took the bag from me and then knelt down to my level.

"Right Abbas, you go and sit over on that seat," he said gently, "and save the two seats next to you for Maman and me. We'll just go and check us in."

"Okay, Baba," I said without hesitation and did as I was told. I was getting very nervous now, so mischief and disobedience were far from my mind. I saw them join the queue from my seat. There were about four or five people ahead of them. They were stationary when my father leaned in toward my mother and whispered something in her ear. Suddenly, my mother checked her headscarf to make sure that her hair was not showing. At home, she never bothered with the religious clothing, but in public, it was compulsory. However, she used to push the boundaries to their limits, and this was not a good place to push boundaries, and I think my father was just telling her that same fact.

As the queue progressed forward, I could see my parents chatting between the two of them quite casually. Everything seemed to be running to plan and going smoothly. I then took my eyes away from them for what seemed to be only thirty seconds as I scanned the room. There were huge pictures and posters of Ayatollah Khomeini all over the airport. There were armed soldiers parading around talking to people and generally making their presence felt. Some of these soldiers seemed to be no older than sixteen or seventeen. I saw people saying their good-byes. I saw people laughing and people crying and people in their own pensive worlds. I really did not think that my attention had been away from my parents for too long, but it obviously had.

As I turned my head toward the check-in desk, I noticed that my parents were already at a desk trying to check in. At first, it all seemed normal, but then I saw that everything was not okay. My father and the man behind the desk were in heavy conversation. My father's body language was one of shock and anger. Both men kept looking at my mother every so often and then continued with their point. I could see my mother trying to chip in with an odd comment here and there, but the main participators in this crescendoing argument were my father and the man behind the desk. Eventually, another man approached the desk to help the other man. The argument was getting very ugly when suddenly my father stopped speaking. He put his hand out in acceptance of the situation and walked away with my mother. She was in obvious shock and finding it hard to come to terms with whatever had happened. I wanted to go over and see what was happening, but I thought better of it.

I saw my parents discuss something between the two of them away from the desk. In reality, I saw my father discuss something with my mother, and she was listening. Her face was not getting better though. In fact, she seemed more and more horrified the more my father spoke. Eventually, she began to talk, and she did not seem happy at all. It escalated into shouting when my father suddenly screamed for her to shut up. Everyone heard that scream; the entire terminal turned round to see what was going on. Then my father leaned over my mother's shoulder and whispered something into her ear. He was pointing to the seats, but not the ones near me. My mother suddenly burst into tears and began to walk to the seats my father had pointed to. I suddenly got up and started to walk toward my mother when I noticed a blazing stare from my father. I stopped dead still and saw him gesture me back to my seat.

I was scared, and so I immediately obeyed his order. I went back, but could not take my eyes off my mother. She couldn't look at me. I really wanted to go and did not know what to do.

I noticed my father walk briskly toward the other side of the terminal. I did not know what he was doing. He walked and walked until he got to a phone booth. He then searched his pockets for change. He still did not pick up the receiver; he looked inside his jacket pocket for his phone book and then began to search through it. I was halfway watching him and halfway keeping an eye on my mother in case she would make eye contact with me. However, she was almost hysterical; I had never seen her like that, even at her mother's funeral. My father looked all around him and with great paranoia as he dialed his digits. I could see him waiting and waiting for a reply. Then with obvious pretence, he smiled as he talked. I could see he was desperate as he was trying very hard. It was like seeing him trying to sell something, only if I could have heard what he was trying to sell. He smiled again and again while talking. Nevertheless, at all time his eyes were searching around, making sure he was not being watched or overheard. Then as his conversation progressed, he looked at me as he talked. I sensed that he was talking about me, but I was paranoid and scared. I just didn't know what was happening.

He finished his conversation and then slowly put the receiver down. He began to walk back toward us, but with nowhere near the same urgency as he walked away. His eyes were everywhere, and his mind was ticking away in his usual stressed manner. I think now he was walking slowly because he was trying to buy time for himself and think through his plan. It was an eternal walk, but as he drew nearer, it was apparent that he was coming to me rather than my mother.

My father came and sat next to me. He did not say anything at first. He was like a stranger. After crossing his legs, he got out his beads and breathed out a sigh of relief. Then he thought for a while as he played with them. I was too scared to say anything. Suddenly he turned to me and talked to me like an adult as much as he could. He took a deep breath before starting to talk.

"They won't let your mother out," he said very calmly and factually.

"Why?" I asked.

"Some technical issue. It's all crap," he said casually, as if talking to his drinking buddy. "It's just a trick to try and keep you here."

"Oh," I said in shock, "so are we going home?"

"Well," he replied hesitantly, "I've been thinking. They're saying that they won't let your mother out, but they're not saying that they won't let you out."

"So?"

"Well that means that you can still go, Abbas."

"What, alone?" I asked almost joking.

"I'm not telling you to go, Abbas, but I'm asking you," he said very calmly. "If you stay, you will probably go to war. I'm not saying you will die, but there is a good chance. However, if you go to Turkey, you have a chance at a life that I can't give you, Abbas. Obviously if it doesn't work out, you can come back. There will be no shame in that—at least you would have tried."

He meant what he said. He really was giving me the choice, but in Persian culture when your father asks you a question like that, you tend to say yes. I really felt I had to go, or I was being told to go. So I just nodded to confirm that I would go, as I didn't have the gall to say it.

"Good lad," he said. "You're a Kazerooni through and through." I just smiled in order to stop myself from crying.

"Right," he said, "because you're only seven years old, you can't just get on a plane. That's why I made that call. I have a friend in Istanbul who will pick you up pretending to be your Uncle Farhad. I won't tell you his real name, as I don't want you to mess it up."

"How will I recognize him, Baba?" I asked.

"Good question," he said, "but I thought of that. I told him to have a large piece of card with your name on it and say that he wrote it for the benefit of the air hostess."

"Okay, so he'll pick me up for sure?"

"Yeah. When you see him, run up to him as if you know him really well, and give him a kiss," he instructed.

"Then what?"

"He should take care of you as he owes me a favor from way back in the olden days." He then reached inside his jacket pocket and took out an envelope. He put it in my hands and still clenched the envelope as he did.

"Inside this envelope, Abbas," he said, "are 1701 US dollars. That is my entire life. Everything we have sold over the last month is inside it. This is now yours," he said, as he paused. "Look after it with your life, and give yourself a start not every child in this country gets."

"I will, Baba," I said softly, trying not to cry. "I promise."

"Good boy," he said with a smile of love and admiration. "I'm very proud of you. You're very brave. Now sit here for a second while I try and check you in." I watched him go over to the desk, which now had no queue at all. This time he had no problem, but I could see that the man behind the desk was surprised as well annoyed as my father had loopholed him. That was so much in my father's character to get the last word. He was a very proud man.

He returned with a big gloating smile on his face. As he reached me, he became serious again. "Remember all that I have taught you," he said like a teacher. "Always think before you do or say."

"Yes, Baba."

"And call me as soon as you arrive, okay?"

"I will."

"Now is the time you have to be a man, my son," he said very formally. "Go and say good-bye to your mother, but please do not cry, as she's very upset. Okay?"

"Okay," I said, trying to hold back all my feelings. I didn't think I was going to be able to hold back the tears with my mother. This was not an ordinary good-bye. My mother was the person I loved most in the world, the person who had brought me up. I slowly walked over to her, where she still sat crying.

"I have to go now, Maman," I said. It was so painful trying not to cry. I was stood next to her stiff, and my eyes were filled with tears, and all I was thinking about was trying to stop them from rolling down my cheeks. "Good-bye, Maman."

My mother held me so tightly that I could barely breathe, but it was a hug that said so many words. She was crying so much, and I felt so guilty for not showing as much emotion as I would have liked.

"Good-bye, my darling," she said. "I love you so much . . . I love you more than anything in this world, Abbas. You know that, right?"

I just nodded, still trying to remain in control.

"I'm so sorry you're going alone, but I promise to join you as soon as I can. I'll try and be there for your birthday in a week."

"Come on, Abs. We've got to get you through the gate," my father said from a

distance.

"Now you look after yourself" were my mother's last words. As I walked away from her, I saw her fall to her knees crying inconsolably. At the gate, when the airhostess was about to take me, my father turned to me and looked at me straight in the face. He then offered his hand for me to shake it. I shook his hand, and he grabbed it extremely hard.

"Good luck, Son," he said. "Have a good trip." As I walked away from the gate, I couldn't look back as tears were rolling down my cheeks quicker and faster than they ever had before. The airhostess took me to the head of all the queues and straight onto the plane.

I cannot remember very much about that flight. I just remember sitting in my seat and looking out of the window hoping I would get one last look at my parents before taking off. I was crying so hard that I was having trouble breathing. I did not cry loudly, as I did not want to draw attention to myself, but I was certainly close to hysteria. I cried myself to sleep before even taking off, and before I knew it, I was landing in Istanbul, where it was night already.

I sat in my seat on the plane until the airhostess came to get me. I don't remember what we talked about on our brief walk to the arrivals lounge, but I know that I was only giving her yes and no answers. I was more worried about seeing my name on the card and acting in the appropriate manner in order not to give the game away. I was really concentrating at the task ahead and did not notice that we were cutting ahead of all the queues again. Suddenly, we came to the arrivals lounge where my eyes were working overtime. There were many signs and amongst them I spotted a tall man with a dark beard and moustache who was obviously Iranian. He was wearing a black shirt and black trousers with sunglasses still on, even though it was night.

As soon as I saw him holding my name up, I dashed for him. I think he was surprised by what I was doing. I jumped at him and hugged him and gave him the two traditional Iranian kisses and said, "Hey Uncle Farhad, how are you?"

"Good, and you?" he replied, not knowing what I was doing.

The airhostess suddenly appeared from behind with her papers.

"Farhad Kazerooni?" she asked with a smile.

"That's me," he responded with a cheesy look. He took the papers off her and signed them. He then watched her leave with a wishful eye. He stopped and looked at me, and I was looking up at him waiting for instruction.

"Go and swap $20 at the Bureau de Change," he instructed forcefully.

"But my father said that I should swap money on the black market because I'd get a better rate," I said hesitantly.

"Did he now?" he said with an arrogant smile. "Well, he's right, but with what does he exactly expect you to pay for the taxi?"

I didn't say anything or argue and went over to the Bureau de Change. However, as I walked away, I was thinking about what he had said. Why would I need a taxi? I was under the impression that this man would look after me. I put $20 on the counter, and the lady automatically did the calculation and gave me the equivalent amount in Turkish Lira. I slowly walked back toward the man and waited to see what he would do.

"Right, here's a list of the cheapest hotels in Istanbul that you'll be safe at," he said firmly. "Only Iranians stay at these hotels, and everyone speaks Farsi. The taxi rank is over there. Now my number is at the bottom of the piece of paper, but do not call it. I repeat, do not call it unless it's a matter of life and death. Do you understand?"

I was blown away at what this man was suggesting. "Yes," I replied with a look of confusion.

"Good, well off you go then," he said with a smile. I think he must have taken some pleasure from watching me suffer.

"But my father said that you'd look after me."

"Your father says a lot of things. Now I don't have time to stay here and entertain you," he snapped. "Now if you don't go, I will."

The man walked off into the crowd, and before I knew it, I'd lost him. There I was with my suitcase in the middle of Istanbul airport. Suddenly, everything was looking so big and things seemed to move so much more quickly. Only a few hours before I was sitting in another international airport, and it did not seem so immense, because I was with my parents. Now that I was alone, everything seemed so daunting.

I did not know what to do. I was not aware that I was crying until I saw the tears hit my shoes. Even with all the lights that are in an airport, the night looked dark and the air seemed thick. I wiped my eyes and tried to sort out in my head what I wanted to do. I just wanted to be with my parents, but the reality was that I was alone in a foreign land at the age of seven, and I did not speak their language. I was quite simply terrified.

CHAPTER 4

My sobbing was mistakable for hyperventilation. I was breathing deeply and quickly. I just didn't know what to do, I was scared, and I didn't trust anyone. As hard as I wanted to stop crying, I couldn't. I was almost about to resign to the fact that my adventure had already come to a halt. I was about to turn around and go to the Iran Air counter. I looked at it, and there was only a man there. He had a sharp face, with a pointy nose and a long beard. This was really the first time that I used my instincts about people. I did not trust this man and decided against that decision. As I was thinking, I found myself sitting on my suitcase.

I stood up to make a decision when a man brushed past me with all his force. He looked at me and began shouting at me in a foreign language. I just looked at him bewildered as what to say or do. However, as I looked around, I realized that I was right in the centre of the airport and in the way. Immediately, I felt my pockets to see that my passport and money were still there. Then I watched the man walk off to make sure he was not coming back.

Then I struggled with my bag to the side where there was a multitude of seats filled with people sleeping on them. I could not help but notice the congregation of families in their variably sized huddles. The small children no older than myself were doing what they do—annoying their parents, asking when they could leave, and crying at the smallest things. I was not ready to be where I was, to make the decisions that I had to make. That was the hardest thing, making decisions—making decisions and sticking to them. Different scenarios were going through my head. What was I going to do? If I went back, my father would definitely be disappointed in me, and the more I thought about it, the more unrealistic that idea felt to me. So that left two options. I would either have to ask for help or go and make a decision myself. One thing that God blessed me with from an early age was basic logic. Should I have asked for help, I was sure that they would have forced me to go back home and that was no longer an option.

Here I made my very first major decision. I knew that I could not just cry as no one cared. Slowly, I picked myself up and struggled with my bags to the large doors near the taxi rank. I had forgotten that it was night outside. At the airport that did not seem like a factor, as the bright lights hid the daunting elements of the night in a foreign land. I strolled through the doors and moved slightly to the right of the doors. I watched others come and saw what they did. They approached the taxis and very simply got into them. This seemed such a hard task at the time. I didn't want to get into a car with a strange person. I did not want to be robbed of all I had, and I was scared and was not sure whether I was doing the right thing.

All these thoughts were circulating around my head when suddenly I heard "Taxi?" I saw a tall, thin man looking at me. He was commonly dressed in an old checked shirt and beige trousers. His shoes were worn out to scruffy gray state. They must have been black at one time, but that was probably a long time ago. He had graying, curly hair. His face was shaved clean, and he held a friendly smile on his inquisitive face.

"Taxi?" he asked again. I was not sure what I should do, but he was saving me the trouble of having to go them. So I shook my head to confirm.

"Iranian?" he asked.

"Yes," I said.

"Maman . . . ehh . . . Baba . . . where?" he asked in his broken Farsi.

"Not here." I had kept it short on purpose. I did not want to make myself vulnerable, so I kept the information on a need-to-know basis.

"Okay," he said. "Where you go?"

I looked at him one more time before committing myself fully. Then I delved into my denim pockets and reached for the screwed-up list that the man had given to me. I slowly brought it out and handed it to him. The taxi driver smiled to himself as soon as he saw the list. I did not have to say anything else; he just knew what to do. He went to pick my suitcase up when I jumped on it. I was still paranoid that everyone was out to take advantage of me. I was far from relaxed. The taxi driver immediately withdrew his hand from the handle and backed away with a friendly smile.

"It's okay . . . I help . . . only help."

"I'm okay."

"Okay," he said with a smile. "Follow me . . . taxi there." I followed him with the case, trying not to show him that it was heavy for me. As we reached the boot of the car, I was struggling to lift the case when he reached down to help me. This time I allowed him. He smiled at me as he showed his pleasure at my small gesture of trust. I pretended it was nothing and continued with the task at hand. My instincts were telling me that this was a good man, but I was not sure. I was keen to show that I was not naïve.

In silence, I got into the back seat and the taxi driver came to the side of the car and shut the door after me. The inside of the car smelled of stale tobacco and body odor. A fine, leopard-skin sheet covered the linen of the backseat. Small holes and stains indicated the age of the sheet. In the front, the rearview mirror had some worry beads hanging from it. The driver's seat was covered with another bright sheet. The driver crept inside cautiously and smiled. He switched the car on and began to drive. He stuck his head of the window and began to wave and shout in order to get out of his spot onto the main road. He was a seasoned professional, and from his gestures and posture, he felt at home behind his steering wheel. As he worked, with the car out of the perimeters of the airport, both of us sat in silence. I was not sure if he knew where he was taking me, and he understood exactly what I wanted, but I dared not speak. I was daring myself to say something, but kept chickening out at the last moment. Eventually, I built up the courage to say something by the time we were away from the airport.

As I was about to speak, the driver looked at me through the rearview mirror and interrupted my intention. "What is your name?"

"Abbas," I said in a monotone manner.

"Meeting you nice, Mr. Abbas. My name . . . Ahmed." He was stunned at my silence and yet continued to smile at me through the mirrors. He could see how nervous I was. He was about to speak but then changed his mind in order to choose his words carefully.

"We go to . . . err . . . different hotels . . . check price, yes?"

"Yes." I was quite amazed at how he knew this, but I tried hard not to let him know that fact. I was very much on my guard. I wanted to look out of the window to see what Istanbul had in store for me, but Ahmed had engaged me in a conversation. I had to concentrate on what he was saying, as I did not want to miss a thing in case he wanted to swindle me.

"I speak good Farsi, yes?" I shook my head to indicate this. I had wondered how he was able to speak Farsi. "There are lots Iranians here . . . I learn lots . . . err . . . how you say . . . many customers are Iranian."

"How many?" I inquired. I had heard this from my father, but I did not know how many exactly.

"They say half to one million."

"One million?"

"Yes," Ahmed replied with a wry smile.

"That is a lot." I could not believe it. Suddenly, I realized that I was happily talking to Ahmed and had brought my barriers down very easily. On the inside, I was extremely angry with myself as this was this early on, and I was trusting people very easily. During this silence, Ahmed felt that there was something wrong with me, and so he tried to continue the conversation so that he could build up more trust with me.

"That is how I know what you want," he said waiting for a response. He saw that he did not get one, and so he continued, "The hotels—most Iranians come with similar list—these hotels are famous in Istanbul for Iranians. Taxi drivers know them very good." I looked at him through the mirrors trying to catch his eyes, but I couldn't. Ahmed was on a roll and was happy that his Farsi was not letting him down. "We go look. Ahmed help find good deal, yes?"

"Thank you," I said. He really was trying to help, but I would see soon enough how helpful he would be. There was another long silence as Ahmed drove for another ten minutes. All I could think about was where we were going and whether I would get a good deal or not. My mind would drift to the image of my mother crying at the airport and falling to her knees. That sight would stay with me for the rest of my life. The thought of her finding out what happened at the airport in Istanbul scared me. I knew that she would be devastated. She would find out soon enough, but how was I to ease the news? All these things were running through my little head; they were so different from the thoughts I was having three weeks ago.

The only adult thoughts that I ever had prior to my trip to Istanbul were about money. I had a scheme a week. I realized there and then that my life was not going to be a normal one from that point forward.

My role and existence had changed dramatically, and I had to adapt swiftly or I would not survive. As I was in my own little world, Ahmed made a long reach to his glove compartment in front of the front passenger seat. This brought me out of my reverie, and I jumped at his action. I was wondering what he was looking for; it could have been anything from a toothpick to a gun. My heart was racing when Ahmed turned around with a big smile with a photograph. He handed it to me.

"My family," he said proudly, "they live in village far away. My son next to me . . . he . . . your age."

I could see what he was trying to do, but it worked as it made me feel easier. I liked the fact that he had his own son and the probability of him not harming me was ever increasing. For another ten minutes, I sat nervously in the back of the taxi listening to Ahmed's pigeon Farsi tour of Istanbul. Usually, I would have found it highly entertaining, but I was in my own little world. I was wondering how the hotels would be and if they would take me seriously. Eventually, Ahmed took a sharp left turn from one of the main streets into a side road. It was not lit and the atmosphere immediately changed. I felt the inside of my stomach coming up. Had I misjudged Ahmed? My father had told me of terrible stories about children being killed for their organs and other horrible scenarios to make me aware of the dangers that I could face. I was not sure whether to say anything or let him carry on. Once again, I had built up the courage to say something when Ahmed took another sharp turn, but this time to the right. As I jilted, I noticed a distant lit-up building in the otherwise dark shadows of this run-down road. Graffiti covered the walls, random drunk or high souls hobbled along the pavements, and each had his own little stare that terrified my imagination and me.

Ahmed stopped the car next to the lit building. A small neon sign indicated that it was a hotel. Ahmed looked at me but said nothing. I stared at him for an awkward three or four seconds. Then Ahmed gently raised his hand to indicate that I should go in if I wanted to check the prices. I did not want to show how scared I was, and so I decided to go for it. I opened the door gently and then looked back at Ahmed.

"I wait here . . . yes?" he said gently.

Then I thought about my things. My suitcase was in the boot of the car and my other bag was in the back of the car with me. I could not take the bags, but then the most important things like the money and my passport were on me. I decided to risk it. I nodded to Ahmed that I would be back soon. I got out of the car, and immediately the smell of wet coal hit me hard. It was truly pungent. A cold breeze went up my spine as I slowly climbed the small stairs into the makeshift lobby of the hotel. I opened the door to find a smoke-filled room with a small reception. Tacky plastic plants were scattered around the circumference of the small room. The windows were so dirty that I could not see outside onto the road. A sweaty unshaved man sat behind the counter. He wore a thin cotton shirt with old trousers. He had his feet up on the desk but had no shoes or socks on. The smell was almost unbearable. A small, old rug lay on the concrete floor, which I guessed acted as a carpet. I looked at the man, but he did not seem to react. I looked again, when suddenly, in a sharp and abrupt tone. he said something to me in Turkish.

"I don't understand Turkish," I said. "Do you . . ."

"Ah, Iranian, yes?" he said with a cheesy smile. He took his cigarette and took a deep puff as I nodded to confirm my nationality. "It's okay. I speak Farsi," he said, as if he could already hear the ching ching of his cash register in his head.

"How much is it for a single room?" I asked very quietly. I lacked any confidence that I needed to be negotiating with a man like this. He looked at me, and after a brief pause, he took another puff of his cigarette. He stubbed it out and leapt to his feet so that he towered over me. He was a huge man, very fat and extremely intimidating. For the first time, I saw his sharp, stained teeth, which revolted me. I had to hold it together, as this man could have easily been dangerous to me.

"How long are you staying?"

"I don't know," I said. Once again he paused to think. I wanted to know what he was staring at and what he was thinking, but all he gave away was his sly, pretentious smile, which quite frankly irritated and horrified me.

"I see," he said. "Well I can't give you price for single, you share with your mother, yes?"

Thinking back on it, he was being clever, but at the time, I could not see his angle.

"No, it's just me," I said quickly. My patience was running out. He was annoying me, and I was halfway thinking about the meter running on the taxi.

"Okay," he murmured as he lit another cigarette. "I can give you good price of 2000 Lira a night."

As he said this, I was about to respond when I heard "Give boy break . . . this no Hilton, my friend."

It was Ahmed. He stood at the lobby door. I looked at him, and he gave me a little wave to show me that it was going to be okay.

"Who are you?" the man asked as if Ahmed had killed his mother.

"A friend," Ahmed responded as cool as a cucumber. "Now you give good price, or we go other hotel." The man sat down on his chair and mumbled something in Turkish at Ahmed, which I later found out to be an offer of 9000 Lira a night.

"Abbas," Ahmed said with a wry smile, "we look different hotel, my friend." He guided me out of the hotel, and I was feeling quite smug that I had already made a good friend. As I was thinking this, I realized that I had misjudged the steps and fell down all of them right to the bottom. I could not bare the pain, but there was no way that I was going to cry. I stood up straight away and laughed at myself the way one does in that situation. However, my back was really hurting me. I opened the taxi door and got in. I was relieved to be out of that hotel and even happier to cushion my back. Ahmed could tell I was in pain, but like the man that he was, he did not let on.

I was already late at night in Istanbul. I remember looking at my Casio watch after leaving the first hotel, and it read something like 11:20 p.m. I was scared at what my parents would think too. I was worried about too many things rather than concentrating on one task at a time.

"Next hotel," Ahmed said, "is very near."

"Okay," I responded. I was tired, and I knew that we had to look at least five or six more hotels before I could make a decision. Once again, the concept of premature adulthood and responsibility were not things that I was too happy about. Ahmed was going round the back streets of the Asian quarter of Istanbul in total darkness apart from the lights of the cars that were traveling on these roads. I had given Ahmed a lot of trust now, and he could have taken me anywhere, and I would not have questioned him. At that age, I was always proud of my perspicacity, but only now in reflection do I realize how naïve I really was.

We traveled for only two minutes when Ahmed took one of his

customary right turns onto a long, straight road. The road was not lit, but I could see sirens of police cars and bright torches in the distance. Ahmed immediately slowed down and rolled toward the light. Obviously, the hotel was in that direction. As we grew nearer, it became apparent that the police activity was outside the only well-lit building on the street, the hotel. As we grew within twenty feet of the activity, I saw that the police had taped off the surrounding vicinity of the hotel. This made it possible for only Ahmed to get past the tape, as the road was already narrow. He had to slow down. There were four or five policemen, one of which was waving Ahmed past. I could not help but look past the waving policeman. Behind him lay a man of around forty, bleeding motionless. His face was sliced, and he had obviously been beaten and stabbed. He lay right in front of the hotel. There were people in the lobby window trying to get a peek at what had happened. I saw a child crying with his mother, as she tried to comfort him on a sofa. This image is one that I carry with me to this day. I can remember wanting to be physically sick. Previously, I had been scared and nervous, but my nerves were taken to a different level. Honestly, I just wanted to be with my parents. I felt vulnerable and scared, and I knew that I could not protect myself fully. Suddenly, it dawned upon me that I had to go into the hotel to get a quote. However, this was the last thing that I wanted to do. I noticed that I was sweating heavily, and yet I was cold. I wiped my head and was trying hard to resist the temptation of crying.

As the car pulled away from the site, Ahmed turned around and looked at me. "We go different hotel, yes?"

"Yes," I murmured quietly. I could not even look at Ahmed as I said that word, as I knew that I would have burst out into tears. I was determined to keep any little respectability that I still had with Ahmed. He might not have been the most educated man or the richest man that I have encountered, but he was most certainly a gentleman in my eyes.

"Next hotel distant, but Ahmed get there fast," he said with a smile trying to make me feel better. As he said this, an ambulance with fill sirens accelerated past the taxi. Both Ahmed and I were silent as we observed their vain attempts to get to the corpse.

We drove for another fifteen or twenty minutes with Ahmed going through his repertoire of clean jokes in Farsi trying to cheer me up. However, nothing was going to get the image of that man out of my mind. I could not smile at anything. My heart would not slow down, no matter how hard I tried to relax. Eventually, Ahmed gave up on me as we drove silently. I dared not look up as I was scared at what I would see. It was not quite the introduction I had expected from this anciently famous city. I had no choice but to look up when I felt the car come to a halt. As I looked up, I saw a disappointed look on Ahmed's face. I did not know why he was looking at me like that, when suddenly he raised his hands to point outside his window. I had no idea of our location, but the street looked as filthy as the last. I saw the hotel that he had brought me to. At first, I thought he was looking at it like that because it was dirty again, but I had expected that. So I looked again only to see a small neon sign in the window flashing FULL. In my little way, I let out a little sigh.

"Big breath for Little Man!" Ahmed said with a smile. I just shrugged my shoulder not knowing when my luck was going to change.

"Next?" inquired Ahmed. I just nodded my head to say yes. I had another sneaky peak at my Casio, and it was well past 12 a.m., which meant that it was even later in Iran. My parents must have been so worried, as they had heard nothing from me. The arrangement was that I was to call once I arrived at the man's house. Yet obviously there would be no house. I was thinking that I would be ordered to return once they heard the news. We could buy everything back and have our old lives back. At that particular moment, nothing seemed more pleasing for me.

Considering the night I had had, it was about time that the spectrum of fate would throw me a piece of luck. However, this was Istanbul; you just never knew. I was learning this extremely quickly, which was important because children have a tendency to get their hopes up and the disappointment can be painful. It was good that I was learning this lesson with something that was not as big as other things in the bigger picture. Eventually, we came to another hotel on what seemed like a road identical to all the other roads that we had seen. It was hard to see what it was really like as it was late and the road was not lit. Even the hotel was badly lit, probably because it was so late. However, right from the start, the place had a better feel to it than all the previous stops. The road still had its needles on the ground, the graffiti on the walls, and the random drunk punters, trying to make their way. Yet right from the start it felt right.

Ahmed stopped the car, and we both got out without looking at each other. I was so glad that he was with me. I climbed the three or four steps into the hotel. Again, the lobby was small and dingy. However, it seemed cleaner than the other lobby we had been in. The few plants that decorated the lobby were real; they were in desperate need of watering, but they were real none the less. Reception was empty, and so I rang the small bell that was on the desk. I could barely see the other side of the counter as it was too high for me. I reached and put the bell back when a tall, thin man came out of what looked like a small kitchen. He looked tired and had not shaved for the entire day, but he had what seemed like friendly eyes. He was wearing a cheap beige suit and a sweat-stained shirt. His tie was halfway down his neck, and his shoes were old, even though they were polished clean. The man forced a smile to welcome us, but it was obvious that he was trying.

"Hello," he said in a surprisingly deep voice. "How can I help you?" He immediately seemed to have more power as soon as he opened his mouth. Of course, he was speaking in Turkish, but I think he knew that I was Persian.

"Do you speak . . ."

"Farsi? Of course I do. In fact, I speak it very well!" His words were more in humor rather than arrogance.

"Do you have any single rooms available?"

"Single?" he asked as he looked at Ahmed.

Ahmed returned the glance. "He's not with me," he said coolly, as if there was nothing wrong. "I'm just a friend."

"I see," the receptionist said. "Well, in that case, yes, I do. However, I need money in advance, as too many of you Persians leave without settling."

"Okay," I said, "but how much per night?"

"Eighty-five hundred Lira, and if you stay more than two weeks, it goes down to 8000."

"How about 6500 and 6000?" Ahmed asked.

Then the receptionist said something to Ahmed in Turkish, and Ahmed responded. Then the man just looked at me and said, "Okay, but do you have any money?"

I didn't know what to do, and so I looked at Ahmed as if he

could help me. He nodded to me to confirm that it was okay to tell him. Therefore, I, in turn, looked at the man and nodded at him. However, nothing seemed to happen. The receptionist kept looking at me as if he expected me to do something. Then when he realized that I had not caught on, he said, "You have to pay week by week—in advance."

I looked at Ahmed again, not knowing if this was standard procedure.

"It is best deal you get, Little Man," he said. "It late, and I have to go see family now. I go get bags."

So I dug into my pockets, reaching for the bundle of dollars, and with my little fingers, I negotiated one bill away from the rest of the pile. I just hoped it was a fifty rather than a $100 bill. Luckily for me, it was a $50 note. So I reached forward with the note to the receptionist whose eyes had immediately lit up. I looked at him and very softly spoke to him. "Keep this until tomorrow, when I will give you Lira. Then you give me back my dollars."

"That is fair."

Then I turned to Ahmed and said, "How much for you?"

"It is okay, Little Man. You need lots help, and I want to help little," he said with smile. The receptionist could not believe what he had heard. He was desperately trying to show that he was not listening, but he was fooling no one.

"No, Ahmed, you take some money," I said. "How much?" Ahmed could see that I was serious and wanted to give him something.

"How about 1000 Lira?"

I reached into my pockets and took five hundred Liras and handed it to him. Ahmed smiled as he saw my gesture. He did not say good-bye, but he did wave at me. He turned toward the door and began to leave before I interrupted him, "Ahmed?"

He turned once again to face me. "Yes?"

"I just wanted to say . . . well . . ."

He then broke off my sentence. "I know, Little Man, I know," he said with a dignified smile. "It has been pleasure for Ahmed." He then turned around, walked out of the door, and got into his taxi without once looking at me again. Through the lobby window, I watched his car drive into the distant night. That was the last time I saw that man, but I thank God that I had the pleasure of his company for a brief period on that particular night.

I turned around from the window to see my receptionist smiling at me. I immediately thought he was a good man, but he looked like he was a little crazy. Not crazy in a sense that he could kill me at any time, but just a little in his own world. He looked like he had crazy ideas, which immediately warmed me to him. I did not know what made me think that, but he just had a look. From a young age, I had become very instinctive about people, and as it turned out, I could not have been more right about this man. I walked up to reception where had adopted his position behind his desk. I looked at him wanting my room key, but I did not say anything. Suddenly, the penny dropped, and he jumped to his feet with a laugh, "Ah, yes, let me show you to your room. You're on the second floor."

"Thank you."

"By the way, my name is Mourat."

CHAPTER 5

Mourat led me up the dark and damp stairs covered in dirty green carpet. We walked through a dim corridor to room 201—what was to be my home for the foreseeable future. He turned the key and opened the door only slightly so that I could still not see inside. "Good night," he said. "Abbas, is it?"

"Yes," I replied. "Good night, Mourat." I watched him whistle to himself as he walked back down the corridor and down the stairs the way that we had come. I almost didn't dare open that door, but I was tired. So I lifted my bags and pushed the door with my foot. The door opened up to reveal a tiny room encapsulated by a queen bed in the center. There was a bedside table on either side of the bed at the far end of the room. Around the bed was approximately one meter of room to the wall. The door faced the foot of the bed and a small cupboard was to the right of the door at the foot of the bed. It had a sliding door so that you could open it. There was a small window to the right of the room as you looked at it from the door. It had mold around the frame and dull gray curtains. The room was damp, and I felt a chill as I stood looking at it in amazement. I was thinking that I had only seen sights such as this in movies, when a cockroach got my attention to the left of the bed next to a door. I had not opened this door yet, and I dared not. I patted the bed linen only to feel dampness again. I could see stains all over the sheets; they were different colors and different shapes making my imagination overload. There were plenty of crimson stains making me feel sick. I didn't just feel sick; I felt like I had to be sick.

Suddenly, I opened the door to the left of the bed and ran inside to find a filthy bathroom. I headed straight for the toilet and was sick until I had nothing left inside me. I remember I was crying and being sick at the same time. How I wished my mother was there rubbing my shoulder and back trying to make me feel better. I kept retching, and small volumes of yellow bile would engulf the toilet basin. The back of my throat was hurting, and I just remember the hanging pungent smell of my sick encircling the bathroom. I kept flushing the toilet, but still random pieces of orange sick, not too dissimilar to chunks of carrot, kept reappearing.

Eventually, I gave up and raised my head to see what the bathroom was actually like. It was quite repulsive. The redbrick colored tiling mixed with the patches of yellow paint covering random areas of the walls made me feel nervous. A freestanding shower stood above me. There was a huge plug in the centre of the slightly sloping floor. I noticed that the floor tiles were also stained with all sorts of colors. Then I noticed a sharp object poking its way through the large plug. I bent slightly over to see what it was. It looked like a used siring needle, which I knew was bad news. Therefore, I went to the bin and took out the liner. I then used it as a glove and very carefully picked up the needle, and then I turned the liner inside out so that the needle was at the bottom of the bin. In the whole process, I was making sure that the needle did not make contact with my skin or pierce my skin. I then washed my hands for what seemed like forever. I soaped my arms up to the elbow like a surgeon. I noticed two or three more cockroaches in the bathroom walking around the edges of the room. I just did not know how I was going to cope with all this. I kept finding myself in a state of tears and then having to wipe them away to solve my next little task, and there seemed to be a never-ending list of problems for me. The first night never seemed like it was going to end.

I made my way to the main room and sat on the bed as I thought about my next move. I lifted my case onto the bed, opened it, and started to put all the clothes in small piles onto it. I had piles of socks, pants, trousers, jeans, T-shirts, shirts, jumpers, and two pairs of shoes as well as the ones I had on. As I looked inside the small cupboard to see where each pile would go, a loud noise caught my attention from outside. It immediately made me jump, and my heart must have missed a few beats. Someone was shouting from outside and his voice was echoing around in the street. I dared myself to creep to the window, and I decided to take a small peek. I could not see very well, as it was so dark, and there was hardly any light outside. What I could make out was a man stumbling around outside with what seemed like blood all over his face. He was shouting like a wild animal. He kept falling over, but when he found any items on the ground like bottles or cans or stones, he would just pick them up and throw them at the houses and the buildings.

Eventually, he threw a stone through a glass window, and within seconds, a light was on. A man put his head out and started to shout at the man in Turkish. The man shouted back at him, and they seemed to be really angry with each other. The man downstairs once again picked up an object and threw it at the window. The man inside suddenly disappeared. I thought the incident was finished, and as I was about to get back to my clothes, the man from the house re-emerged on the street with a big stick or a bat. He ran after the man who could barely walk and beat him into a pulp. I could not take my eyes off the incident, but how I wished I had. I looked on as the man bled silently on the street. Yet the other man seemed to have no mercy; he kept swinging his bat and shouting, and I could hear every thud as his victim lay bleeding. I wanted to shout for someone to help, but I dared not make a squeak. Silent tears rolled down my cheeks as I watched on. I turned away and realized once again how vulnerable I was in this foreign land. How I wished my father . . . and there it was. I suddenly remembered that I had not called my parents.

I looked at my watch, and it read 3 a.m. local time. It must have been dawn in Tehran. Honestly, I did not want to leave my room, but there was no telephone in my room. I slowly turned the key in my lock and opened the door. Then I locked the door behind me and began slowly to go downstairs. I was so scared, and I could not take the image of the man beating the other out of my head. I had witnessed two violent images in one night, and it was far from what I was used to. I walked slowly to begin with, and then decided that I should run downstairs. I ran down the two flights of stairs as quickly as I could until I reached reception again. Mourat was there halfway asleep, and he seemed more than surprised to see me again this soon.

"Something wrong?" he asked.

"No, I just need to . . ."

Then he cut me off. "Did you see what happened outside?"

"No," I said pretending all was well. I don't quite know why I lied, but I did not want to talk about it.

"Oh, so what is wrong?"

"Nothing, I just want to use the telephone," I said. "Is that possible?"

"Yes, of course," he said a little distracted. "You give me the

59

number and then when I connect, you pick up in one of those cubicles." He was pointing to three little cubicles at the far end of the small lobby.

"Okay," I replied, "can they call me too?"

"Yes."

"Okay, can I have the number for here, please?"

"Sure." As he pulled out a card with the hotel details, he said, "Do you still want to make a call?"

"Yes," I said as I looked at him. He looked right at back at me, trying to figure out if I had been crying. I don't think he could tell, as I had washed my face, and I was acting more confident that I actually was. "Can I have a piece of paper?"

He handed me a piece of paper and a pen, and I wrote down my home number for him.

"Shall I wait here or in the cubicle?"

"Wait here. If I connect, I'll wave and you go into cubicle one."

I looked at my watch again as Mourat dialed. I was so scared to tell my father what had happened. I did not know what to tell him. Which parts of the night should I omit? I was sure that if I told him half of the happening that he'd have me on the first plane home anyway. There would be no need to worry him more than be necessary. I had my plan all together, and I thought I knew what I was going to tell him.

Suddenly, Mourat started to wave at me, and I could hear him saying, "I have international call for you from Istanbul." The phone in cubicle one started to ring. It was much louder than I had anticipated, which made move faster as I did not want to disturb anyone at that time of the night. I breathed out one more time as I picked the phone up.

"Hello?" I said hoping for a friendly voice.

"Abbas, is that you?" I heard my father say. I could feel the angry and worrying vibrations through his intonation.

"Yes, Baba. It's me," I said softly.

"Where have you been? Why didn't you . . ."

"Baba," I screamed, "take this number down and call me back at my hotel."

"Hotel? What hotel?" he demanded.

"Baba, take it down, call me back, and I'll tell you." I could not believe that I had spoken to my father like that, but I knew deep down that I was right. Suddenly, I felt a rush of power, and it felt quite good. I still wanted to go home, and I was still scared, but never in my wildest dreams did I ever think I could ever get away with shouting at my father. I gave him the digits and put the phone down. I felt a little more confident about talking to him now, but I still expected a bombardment of questions. The Spanish inquisition was yet to commence!

I stayed in my cubicle and waited for the phone to ring again. Sure enough, within minutes the phone rang again, and before either of spoke, I felt the wrath of my father's fury. I didn't quite know whom he was angry at, but I knew enough to be aware of what I said!

"Hello?"

"Abbas? Why are you in a hotel?" he asked firmly.

"Well . . ."

"What happened to the man who was supposed to pick you up?"

"As soon as he signed me in, he told me to swap $20 from the bank. I told him that you'd told me not to, but he insisted."

"Okay," he said curiously, "so then what happened?"

"Well, I thought he was going to take me with him like you said he would, but he gave me a list of hotels and told me where I could find a taxi." I paused for a while, and I could feel my father getting more angry as the silence grew, so I decided to continue with my account. "I didn't know what to do, Baba. If I had asked for help at the airport, I was sure they'd send me back."

"Okay, so what did you do?"

Suddenly I heard the ever graceful voice of my mother in the background. "Don't be so hard on the boy. He's trying his best. Is he okay?"

"Just let me deal with this, Marzieh, will you?"

"Baba, is that Maman? Can I speak to her?" I asked. Her voice was the only thing that was going to soothe me a little.

"No you can't," my father retorted. "You just tell me what happened next."

"Well, like I said, I was scared to ask for help at the airport, and so I went and found a taxi and started to look at prices from the list that man gave me."

"That idiot!" he shouted. "If I get my hands on him . . ."

"Karim . . . ," my mother firmly interrupted.

"So what are these hotels like, Abbas?"

"They're okay, Baba," I said trying to sound like I meant what I was saying, "but I got a good rate I think. The taxi driver helped me."

"What taxi driver?"

"The taxi driver that drove me from hotel to hotel?"

"He's gone, right?"

"Yes, Baba. He's gone," I said firmly.

"So how much is the hotel?" I hesitated for a while, as I did not know if my deal was good or not. So I just crossed my fingers and hoped for the best.

"Six thousand, five hundred Lira a night for the first two weeks and then 6000 Lira a night after that."

There was a pause as my father punched the numbers into head in the early hours of the morning. The silence was killing me as this was my first test, and I did not want to have failed.

"That's not bad, Abs." Music to my ears! From my father, that was a compliment.

"So what should I do next, Baba?" There was a sudden silence when I heard my parents arguing between themselves.

"Just let me speak to him for a few seconds, Karim," I heard my mother beg. "Please?"

"The boy's traumatized; I don't need him being more upset."

"He's my son too," she screamed, as if she were on the phone too. "Let me speak to him now."

"Not until you're calm, woman."

"I am calm," she screamed. "Who do you think you are?"

"Baba," I said quietly, but there was no response as they continued to argue. "Baba!" I called a little louder.

"What?" he snapped.

"Why can't I speak to Maman?"

"Because you will upset each other."

"Well, I am going to see you soon anyway, aren't I?" There was a silence. I could not quite understand it, as I was more than sure that he was going to tell me what to do to return as soon as I could. However, the longer the silence was, the more I felt that this would not be his response.

"Baba?"

"Yes?"

"I am coming home, right?"

"I don't think you should, Abs," he said softly. I didn't say anything, but it was like I had been told that my worst nightmare had come true. I could not believe that my father was going to allow me to stay in this hell. I felt tears roll down my cheeks in silence once again. I did not want my father to tell that I was crying, and so I just didn't speak. This silence was the longest of them all. I think my father was trying to choose his words carefully in order to make me feel better. However, at that particular moment, I needed more than a few words. I needed more confidence, I needed encouragement, and most of all I needed my parents. Alternatively, I needed a miracle.

"Abs?" he said to no response, "you still there?"

"Yeah," I gently groaned trying to hide my melancholy.

"You're going to have to be strong now, Abs," he said desperately. "You're going to have to be a man." What could I possibly say to this? I could not tell him that I couldn't cope because I was scared that he'd be disappointed in me. All my life he had spoken to me saying that he didn't want to be disappointed by me, and that I was his last chance. If I didn't try as he was asking, I thought that life would not be the same once I returned. So with pride, I held my tongue, though deep down I did not know how I was going to survive. I did not know what to do, I did not who trust, and from what I had seen that night, I did not know if I was going to live to see another day. I was quite simply terrified. Even though I did not speak the language of defeat, I felt it inside, and so I chose to say nothing.

"Abs?"

"Yeah?"

"You've already shown me you can handle yourself like an adult," he said. I did not know what he was talking about. I was scared to death, and all I wanted was my mother holding me. This was a far cry from adulthood, and yet again, I bit my tongue.

"You got a taxi all the way from the airport and looked around a strange city for a good hotel. It is a really good hotel right?"

"Err . . . I guess," I said, knowing that I could not really go back on what I had previously said.

"And it's in a good area, right?"

"Yeah," I said softly. I had resigned myself to lying to him. It was not worth the both of us feeling bad. I knew from the airport in Tehran that my father carried the responsibility of my safety solely on his own shoulders. My mother had at no stage wanted a part of this. Though my father had never been one for emotions, I liked to think that he was worried about me and felt guilty for sending me alone. I guess that was selfish on my part, but maybe it was due to the fact that he never really told me what he felt about me in contrast to my mother. Thus I could not really tell him how I felt, because I thought that the guilt and burden that he already carried on his shoulders was enough and needed no addition. As an adult, I guess this is one of my proudest aspects of my childhood, having that kind of astuteness at such a tender age.

"Yeah," my father continued, "if you can get a taxi in Istanbul, go round and get prices, and eventually find a good hotel all by yourself, then there's no reason why you can't do everything else by yourself, is there?" I couldn't quite bring myself to answer him. "Is there? Abs?"

"No, Baba."

"Good, then. It's settled." I wasn't sure whom he was trying to kid.

"Baba?"

"Yes?" he said excitedly.

"So what do I have to do exactly?" I asked, hoping that his response would be short, sharp, and not too difficult. Once again, I knew deep down that the reality would be far removed from what I wanted.

"Well you have to get to the British Embassy somehow," he said while thinking at the same time. "There you have to try and get a visa."

"I have to exchange money first, Dad, to pay for the hotel," I said as a matter of fact. "They want payment weekly, in advance, and I've left a $50 deposit until I have Lira. Then I'll get my fifty back."

"Right," then that's what you have to do, "but don't . . ."

"I know, swap it at the bank," I said knowingly. "I'll find a black market dealer like you told me."

"Good lad," he said all excited again, "good lad. I told you that you could do it. Just ask someone Persian tomorrow where they swap their money, and then go and get it from the same place, as you can bet that they've found the best deal."

"Okay," I said, not being sold by his argument, "and at the embassy . . . ?"

"Ah, yes," he cut in again, "at the embassy, you'll find it a little difficult because they don't speak Farsi. They only speak Turkish and English."

"So what shall I do Baba?" There was another silence as he thought about the question as it was a good one.

"Well I'm guessing that there will be some Iranians there as the place is full of us. If that's the case, then ask for help. Never be shy to ask for help; just choose whom you ask carefully, as they may try and take advantage of you."

"How do I know whom I should ask?" I questioned innocently.

"Son, that is a good question," he said very profoundly, "as I'm still trying to work that one out for myself. It's like knowing whom you can trust or not trust. Some people have it in them to know and some don't. It's like a sixth sense, Abs. We'll soon see if you have it in you or not . . . but I think you do."

"I do?"

"I think so, Son," he said. "I think so." For the first time in the conversation, I felt a little better, and yet it seemed such a small thing. It did not take away what I had witnessed or how difficult the following day would be, but my father thinking that I have something that most people do not was a great feeling for me.

"So if I get someone to help me, Baba," I inquired, "what do I tell them at the embassy?"

"The truth, Abs," he said firmly. "Always tell them the truth, because they'll find out, and you'll never get to England."

"Okay."

"Tell them that you had to leave to avoid having to go to war. Tell them that your father believed that the best thing for a child of your age is education, and that you were not going to be allowed to get it in your own country. Tell them that the regime was so determined to keep you for war that they stopped your parents leaving with you. Tell them that you want to go to England to stay with your cousin, Mehdi, who has lived there for fourteen years and has residency. He has agreed to be your guardian. He is a chef, if they need to know that. More than likely, they will need documentation. Write down what they ask for, and I will call you around 9 p.m. your time tomorrow night. You can tell me what the documentation is, and I'll get to you as fast as I can. Okay?"

It seemed so simple to him, but that was a lot of information for me. It was late, I was scared, and yet again, I was scared that I would get it all wrong.

"Okay," I said.

"Abs?"

"Yes, Baba?"

"Be careful, my boy. Don't leave the hotel at night."

"I wasn't going to," I said firmly. Having seen what I had, I would try and avoid leaving the hotel even during the day.

"Good lad," he said, "good lad."

"Baba?" I said gently.

"Yes, Abs?"

"Can I speak to Maman, please?"

"Not tonight, Son," he responded with sadness. He had felt my desperation in my voice and still he said no. "Maybe tomorrow." I had no more energy to argue with him, but I still felt great sadness within me, as I missed my mother more than anything else.

"Okay."

"Now go to bed, Abs," he ordered. "You must be tired."

"Yup, I am. Say good night to Maman for me."

"I will."

"Good night, Baba."

"Good night, Son," he said. "Oh, Abs?"

"Yeah?"

"We're proud of you, Son."

"Yeah." There I put the phone down, not being able to breath. I was so glad that it was late, as I didn't want anyone to see me like this. I had to control myself and be calm before I passed Mourat again. Gently, I opened the cubicle door and crept past reception without being noticed. I walked upstairs with my head down. I remember seeing all the stains and damp parts of the green carpet while dragging myself upstairs. It was late but I didn't feel sleepy.

I opened the door to my room to see my clothes still on the bed. I crept around in the little space available and slid open the cupboard door. I slowly started to put my clothes away without even thinking about what I was doing. All I could think about was finding somewhere to swap money the next day and not getting ripped off. Then I had to find the embassy, and then I had to try and find someone to help me communicate. It was all too much for me, and again, I started to cry. It was a monotonous activity by now, and I was getting fed up of weeping, but I couldn't help it. The tears just rolled down my cheeks, and sometimes I would not know that I was crying until the tears touched a part of my skin where I felt them.

Once my clothes were away, I went to draw the curtains, and once again, I remembered what I had seen earlier. The images just terrified me. I quickly closed the curtains and walked away from the window. I slowly took off my clothes and put on my pajamas. I went to the door and turned off the light. Slowly, I crept the meter to the edge of the bed, but I could not force myself to lie on the bed in the dark. With the loss of my own pride, I turned around and turned the light on again. Once again, I turned toward the bed and crept onto it. I then edged my way to the top end of the bed and drew back the covers. I made my way under the covers to feel a coldness that I had never felt before. The sheets were still damp and the coldness of the night was going through my body. Every little noise was apparent to me. A small draft was whistling through the gaps of the window. The small flaps of the curtains were making me feel as though I were being watched. Every shadow in the room seemed to create the outline of an enormous monster. I felt so tired, but I just did not want to sleep, as I was scared that I would not wake again. Suddenly, I saw my tears hit the sheets that covered my body. I tried to shut my eyes and make myself invisible, but it just didn't seem to work. My crying gradually turned into sobbing, and for the first time in the evening, my crying had become slightly vocal. I just remember crying and crying until I had no tears left; all my energy had gone. I was hungry, I was thirsty, and most of all I was homesick. That night just didn't want to end, and yet after minutes of crying, minutes that seemed like hours, I drifted off to sleep.

CHAPTER 6

I remember waking up the first morning in a haze. I was hoping the previous night had been all a dream, but it wasn't. It wasn't even properly light yet, but the hustle and bustle of the early morning had woken me up. I could not have slept for very long or very deeply. I think I had slept for about three hours. I did not want to get out of bed. I thought to myself that if I just stayed there everything would improve. It was wishful thinking, and I knew it. I had to dare myself to look outside. After what I had seen the previous night, looking out was not such an easy thing to do. I crept out of bed and edged my way to the side of the window and gently lifted the side of the curtain. This way I could look out and not be seen—at least that was what I hoped. I saw a slightly busier street with people dressed in all sorts of attire. My first impressions were not great. The street looked even dirtier than the night before, as it had been hidden by the darkness of the night. There seemed to be litter everywhere, and the smell seemed more apparent; it was strong and pungent. The smell was a mixture of damp coal and rubbish mixed together. The few people who seemed to be up at that time of the morning were all ignoring each other. There was no familiarity with anyone. Some people were dressed in cheap, worn-out suits, some in jeans and leather jackets, and some with ripped-up clothes. Some people seemed to be returning from the previous night. The street and the buildings had a gray atmosphere to them. It was not a bad day outside, but there was a coldness to it. I could not help but have a feeling of foreboding.

I crept away from the window and entered the bathroom the other side of the room. Usually my mother would have to tell me or force me to take a shower in the morning, but I just felt horrible and dirty from the previous night. I wanted to have a shower, and the fact that I did made me feel slightly grown up. On every occasion that I would notice myself doing something that was slightly beyond my years, it would give me confidence. It may seem like a strange thing to say, but these little feelings of maturity were the feelings that carried me through each single day.

I walked into the bathroom, and from the inside, I tried my hardest to lock the door. Unfortunately, it would not lock, however hard I tried. I just did not feel safe, even within the bounds of my room. I shut the door firmly and just looked at it. Realizing that I had no other option, I began to undress. I took off my pajamas very slowly and put them away from the freestanding showerhead so that they would not get wet. Then I located the towel and saw that it was within reach. I had my shampoo and soap with me, and I was ready to go. I turned the tap on, only to hear the loudest howl, which must have echoed throughout the hotel. Slowly, a little water began to drip out, but without any real power. I waited and waited, but the water would not turn warm. I checked the colors on the taps to see that I had turned on the right one on. Sure enough, the red one had been turned. I waited for a few more minutes, and to my frustration, it was still cold. As a last resort, I turned off the red one and turned on the blue tap. Within seconds, warm water was coming out, very slowly. It was not the ideal way to start the day, but I had to clean myself. Methodically, I began to wash my head and body only to notice other unwanted cockroaches running around my bathroom. Though they made my body crawl, even at this early stage I was getting used to them.

I came out of the shower while patting myself dry. Suddenly, I realized how hungry I was. However, I remembered my father telling me that I should only eat once a day, as I did not know how long I was going to be staying in Istanbul. I needed to save my money, but the last time that I had had a real meal was in Iran. I had also missed my meal on the flight to Istanbul, as I had slept all the way. However, I made a decision then and there that I was not going to eat that night because I wanted to reward myself for the day that I was about to have. I had plenty of important business to take care of, and I had little time to eat—at least that was my thinking. Once again, I was trying to kid myself into thinking that I was an adult, which psychologically always worked with me. The funny aspect of it was that I knew what I was doing. I was playing games with my own mind, but the motivation methodology always worked—and it still does.

Once dry, I immediately put on the first pair of briefs that I could find, as I was never comfortable naked in that room. I do not know why, but it made me feel more vulnerable than I already was. As I knew that

I had to exchange money and visit the British Embassy that day, I had to dress to impress. My father had always told me that first impressions go a long way, and that I should try to make the best impression that I could when meeting people for the first time. So slid open the cupboard door and the hunt began. I took out every shirt that I had and inspected each one individually and matched them to the trousers that I had. I remember clearly that the shirt was red and checked and the trousers were beige. I took out my black smart shoes, and with my shoe shining kit, I cleaned them as well as I could. Then I put on all my clothes, made sure that I had my money, and went to open the door. As I was about to open it, I double-checked my pockets to make sure that my money and passport were on my possession, as I did not trust the hotel or anything that was associated with it.

Down the smelly corridors and stairs I went, and I made my way to the reception. The hotel was still silent, and there was no movement anywhere. It was still very early, but I was fully awake. Mourat was asleep behind his desk. His head was in his hands as he snored in little pathetic bursts, while dribbling onto his papers that scattered the desk. I decided against waking him, as I wanted to see if there were any Iranians in the hotel. Therefore, I decided to sit in the lobby and wait. There were a few old sofas next to the phone cubicles to the right of reception as you looked onto the street. I sat there and waited. At first, it was okay, but after about twenty minutes, I began to feel bored. I was taking in my surroundings—the few plants that supposedly decorated the lobby in the very tradition of third-rate hotels in the Asian Quarter. The badly painted walls were a particular feature, as the stains that they were covering up were still visible through the layer of paint that had been allocated. They obviously needed a few more coats, but apparently, the hotel budget did not reach to that. The one thing that the lobby did have going for it was the clean window that looked onto the street. Everything was visible, and it looked like it had been cleaned at least in the last week. It was a huge improvement to the lobbies I had witnessed the previous night. As grotty as the hotel and the area were, this hotel felt okay to me. The lobby made me feel a little better. I did not know what it was, but it had a certain character to it. I actually remember feeling safer there than I did the previous night in my room.

As the boredom grew and the time past, I decided that it was time to write my first letter. It was going to be written to my mother. I snuck up to the front desk where Mourat was still in another land. I saw some paper and a few pens and pencils, and thus I decided to help myself. I did not think that he would mind. So away I went with the first letter that I ever wrote, which went as the following:

Hello Maman,

How are you? I am fine. I am going to the British Embassy today. I am going to tell them that I need a better education. I am going to tell them what Baba told me. He told me that I should never lie to them, because they would find out. You know the program that was on TV a few years ago? The one about my great-grandfather giving money to soldiers to fight the English? Well, I am not sure they will like it if I tell them about our family history. Would it be lying if I did not say anything? Until I get a response from you, I will not say anything. I hope that I get a visa, because I can see cousin Mehdi and tell you how great England is. Will you tell my friends that I beat them there? I just wish that you were here with me. I know that Baba says that I should not say so, but I do miss you, Maman. I wish I could have talked to you last night, but know that I am okay. I am almost eight years old and can take care of myself. After all, like Mamanjoon says, I am a Kazerooni! The hotel is really nice, and Istanbul is a really nice city, but I will see more of it today. I will tell you about my visit to the city and the embassy in my next letter. I have to exchange money before I go to the embassy. Don't worry. I will look for the best rate. Just know that I am okay, and hopefully, I will speak to you tonight.

Good Bye

Your Son, Abbas

After I finished my first masterpiece, I was sat idle again. I also knew that I needed an envelope, but maybe Mourat would give me one. Not long after Mourat's squashed and sleepy face rose from the dead.

"Morning," I said cheerfully.

"Do you know you shouldn't be this happy at this time?" he said sarcastically. I did not quite understand what he was trying to say, but I smiled at him anyway.

"Do you have an envelope I can have?" Without even asking or saying anything, he help up an envelope, and I quickly went to grab it from him.

"Do you want stamps too?"

"Do you have some?" I asked excitedly.

"Sure, just leave the letter with the address on it here, and I will post it for you," his sleepy voice mumbled.

"Thank you," I said, as I ran back with the envelope to write down my address on it.

"So why are you up so early?"

"I have to go to the city and the British Embassy," I said with a little less confidence, "but I just wanted to see if there are any Iranians here that can point me in the right direction."

"You're clever than you look," he said with a smile. It took me a few seconds to work it out, but then I laughed along with him. "I would take you myself as I have to go to the city, but my shift does not finish until around 12. You have to go as early as you can as the queues get long at embassies."

"I know."

"Well, if you hang around here for a while, some of your countrymen and women will surface soon."

"So there are Iranian here then?" I said with real enthusiasm.

"Oh, yeah," he said. I could not figure out if he was happy about it or not, but I did not care, as it helped my cause. Mourat suddenly disappeared as he decided to fall asleep again. So there I was sat again with nothing to do. However, I was really happy that I had written a letter. It was a new experience for me. It was exciting that my mother would read that very same piece of paper with my handwriting on it in a week or so. I guess I was not that hard to please! The next hour must have passed quite quickly, as all I remember doing was thinking about how the day was going to pan out. I was mostly scared about the embassy. I had never been in an embassy before. Would I find someone to help me communicate? If so, what would I say? Would I say the right things? As I was going through various different scenarios and inner monologues, I heard a young Iranian couple walk down the stairs.

"So why do we have to leave this early?" I heard the woman say.

"Because we'll get the best deals—it's that simple," the man responded authoritatively. "If you don't want to come, then don't."

Suddenly they both appeared. They were both in the early thirties, both quite good looking, but something did not seem right about them as a couple. The woman had too much makeup on, and the man could have done with a shave. He had a harder face, and I trusted him less than the woman. Ideally, I would not have talked to either of them. They walked past reception, where I smiled at them. "Good morning."

They seemed quite shocked to see me, but I was obviously Iranian, and so they felt obliged to respond with a chorus like "Morning."

The man's voice was forced, and I felt that he said it more out of courtesy rather than will. The woman, however, had a real genuine smile on her face and wanted to speak to me.

"Are you Iranian?" I asked, knowing full well that they are.

"Yes," the woman replied, "where are you from?"

"Tehran."

"We're from Mashad."

"Oh, I've been there. I went once with my father," I said quite proudly, "but I prefer Tehran." They both smiled; even the man saw the funny side of my comment.

"Are you here on holiday with your parents?" the lady asked.

"No, I'm here alone." My voice was very serious and monotone. Again they both laughed out loudly, thinking that I was joking.

"Really, I am here alone. I have come to get a visa for England."

"Really?" the woman asked.

"Of course not, you silly woman," the man snapped. "He's joking."

"No, I'm here alone. I got here last night, and I was waiting to see if anyone can tell me where I can change some money apart from a bank. I also need to know where the embassy is."

"How much money do you need to change?" the man immediately replied. I looked at him and was not sure if I should answer him or not.

There was an awkward silence, and then the lady rescued me. "It's okay. You don't have to say, Sweetie. Sure we can show you where to go to swap money, but I am not sure where the embassy is, as we are here only on holiday," she said in the sweetest of voices. I could tell that she felt for me. Then I noticed a look from the man trying to suggest that they should disassociate themselves from me.

"If you just give me the directions, I will find it," I said. I was still worried about the embassy, but one out of two was not bad.

"Okay," the man said, "you have to go left as soon as you leave the hotel, and you go straight until you hit the main road. You'll know it's the main road, because it will be much busier and the buildings are nicer. Then turn right toward the big mosque and keep going until you reach a big indoor market. There all the jewelers swap money." I knew that the part about the jewelers must be true, as I remembered my father having told me a similar thing.

"Thank you," I said. "I really appreciate it. Have a lovely day." Then I just got out of my chair and headed out of the hotel. I had not left yet when I heard the woman start shouting at the man. I could see an argument brewing, and it was obvious that it was about me. Therefore, I kept on walking. I kept thinking that with a bit of luck they would follow me and offer to show me personally.

Nothing seemed to happen as I walked, and then suddenly I heard "Hey, kid."

It was the man, with the woman following in hot pursuit. I was trying hard not to show my glee, so I waited on the pavement, pretending I was surprised that they had followed me. I watched them approach.

"Sweetie," the lady said out of breath, "you know what? We are going in that direction, and so we thought we would go all together so that we can show you."

"Oh, thanks," I said, still pretending to be shocked that they had followed me. "I would have been fine though."

"Well, we were going," she responded desperately trying to be nice, "so we thought—why not all go together?"

"Thank you," I said very politely. The man still seemed to hold some reservation about me, and for that reason, he spoke very little.

"So what is your name?"

"Oh, sorry. I am Abbas," I said to the lady.

"I'm Assal, and this is my husband, Ali."

"Nice to meet you," I said to both of them. I stopped walking and offered my hand for a formal handshake. They were both taken back at this gesture, and yet they both complied with a slight sneer.

Suddenly, we hit the main road where I realized I was in a major city. The main road might as well have been a different place. Taxis, cars, and vans all tried to monopolize their little piece of road. Horns were going off at every little incident, and the pedestrians were not much better. The hustle and bustle of a big city had hit home. However, the buildings were far more impressive, and the mosque in the distance, the one we were heading for, seemed to capture the mood of this actually beautiful city. Nevertheless, I was much more scared here, as I felt more vulnerable. I was glad that Assal and Ali were with me. I kept subtly checking my pockets making sure that my passport and money were safe. My paranoia eventually led me to walk with my hands in my pockets. I could not believe how busy this city was. Every so often, I would hear a family walking past and talking in Farsi. It was true; the place was overwhelmed by Iranians. I found it very difficult to cope with the shear size of the city and the number of people pushing past me. My mere insignificance was highlighted for the first time. No one seemed to care, everyone had their agenda, and I was no more than a statistic for the Turkish tourism board. I let Ali and Assal lead the way, and I followed them from an approximate five-meter distance. They seemed very intimate and could not keep their hands off each other. This was unusual behavior in the Iranian culture. I never quite found out what was strange about this couple, but I am still convinced that something was not right. They were either not married, which was the most probable thing, or they were just married and hence very affectionate.

Eventually, we arrived at a huge entrance to an indoor market. It was so high and so deep. It was a long, straight market with little stalls and shops on either side. Every third shop was, of course, a jewelry shop. Then Ali turned to me. "Well, this is it, Kiddo," he said in a patronizing tone. "We usually choose one of these jewelers; they tend to give roughly the same rate."

"Thank you."

Then I saw Assal whisper something in his ear, and he just nodded his head, meaning no.

"We have to be off," he said abruptly. "Good luck, and maybe we'll see you later at the hotel."

"Okay," I said. "I'll see you later." Then they began to walk off, and Assal turned one more time to take a final look at me and gave me a little wave. I was watching them and trying to remember the way that we had come so that I could find my way back. As I was going over all the roads, I looked harder at the market and realized that I had lost Assal and Ali in the crowd. I took a deep breath and knew that my day was about to begin for real. I looked at the first jewelers to my left and walked in. It was actually empty. A bell rang in the small shop as the door opened. It was covered in gold items of variable prices. A man came out from the back. I could tell that he was a good man right from the start. He was dressed very smartly and most of all he had kind eyes. He had a tie on; his shirt was not overly expensive, but well ironed, and it made him look good.   He smiled at me and without prejudice asked me, "How can I help you?"

"You speak Farsi?" I asked.

"Yes, I do," he said.

"How did you know I am Iranian?"

"I can just tell," he said with a smile. "I see enough Iranians every day to tell the difference." I smiled because he had a point. On the way to the market, I had lost count of the number of Iranians I had seen.

"Do you exchange dollars for Lira?"

The man smiled and with a deep, elegant voice said, "Of course, today's rate is 980 Lira per dollar."

I looked at the man, and I was pretty sure he was being fair, but I could not take that chance. So I smiled and said, "Thank you, I will be back in a while."

"No problem," he said, "Take your time."

Even though I didn't buy from him, I got a really gentle feel about that man and his shop. I left the shop and ventured down the market. Once again, this was an overwhelming experience. Every stall-holder was trying to sell his products to me, and the word "no" did not usually exist in their vocabularies. The products varied from backgammon boards to handmade furniture to gold-plated tea sets to cutlery. Everyone wanted a piece of me and my money, and I was determined to ignore them. It was not so easy ignoring everyone and saying no to everyone. They would follow you and tell you jokes and do absolutely anything to sell what they had. This was my first day, and there and then, I decided I hated tourists as they encouraged the stallholders to behave like this. Of course, I had my agenda, and it suited me to hate them!

Off I went into almost every jeweler's shop and asked for the dollar rate. Almost without exception, every shopkeeper spoke Farsi, and their rates varied from 950 to 980. That very first man had given me the equal best rate. To be fair, every other holder had given me a rate near to that, and no one had tried to hustle me, which pleased me somewhat. As I had to go back to the entrance of the market anyway, I decided that I would swap money with the original dealer because I liked him the most, and I seemed to trust him the most too. So I made my way back to the entrance after two hours of walking, dodging, and bartering dollar rates. I had learned, on this little trip, in Istanbul there was no shame in bartering for the price of anything. I opened the shop door only for the bell to ring in its usual manner, only this time the man was not in the back room.

He smiled in his gentle way. "So I gave the best rate, eh?"

"Equal best," I said. "Two others gave me the same rate."

"They were both at the other end of the market, right?" he asked knowingly. He had a gentle glitter in his eyes that I warmed to from the start.

"Yes," I said, halfway shocked. "How do you know?"

"It's my job!" he said with a smile, "but you did come back to me, and for that I want to give you an even better rate, Little Man." This was the second time I had been referred to as "the Little Man," and quite honestly, I liked it.

"What rate?"

"How does 1000 Lira a dollar sound to you?" he asked.

"I'll take it." Then there was a sudden silence as I remembered that I only wanted to swap $50. However, I decided not to say anything, and instead, I got the $50 note out of my pocket and placed it on the counter. The man smiled, and he also decided against saying anything and went to take the money. My hand was still on the note, and as his hand came toward it, my hand did not give way. The man once again smiled and took his hands away and opened his till. He counted out the Lira in front of me and placed it next to my hand. I remember feeling a little embarrassed, and so I slowly took off my hand off the note and took the pile of money. I wanted to count the Lira for myself, but I thought that considering my behavior I should not until I left the shop.

Once we both had our money, he looked at me and said, "You come to me again, and I guarantee the best rate again," he said with a smile. "What do you say?"

I looked at him and kind of shrugged my shoulders to suggest that I could not think of anything better. "Okay."

I was really proud of myself, because not had I only got the best dollar rate in Istanbul that day, but I had made a contact with someone in the field. I could not wait to tell my father all this.

"My name is Hector. If you need help with anything, I'm your man."

"Thank you, Hector," I said very politely. "My name is Abbas." I went to leave when suddenly I remembered something. "Hector?"

"Yes?"

"I want to go to the British Embassy," I said hopefully.

"Okay."

"I don't suppose you know where it is and if there is a bus that goes way?"

Hector smiled and looked at me. Looking back, I think that many people would have asked many questions as why I wanted to go or what my intentions were and so on. Not Hector, like the man that he was, he just told me what I wanted to know.

"It's your lucky day, Little Man, because not only do I know where it is, but I know which bus you need too." He came out from behind his counter and walked to the door. He stopped at the door and then lifted his right hand to point, and then suddenly, he flapped it down. "You know, it is much easier if I just show you."

"Can you do that?"

"Sure," he said as he pulled out a set of keys and locked the door behind him. He then stepped out and shouted something in Turkish across the market to another stallholder who shouted something back him. "The bus stop is only two minutes walk from here."

We walked in the busy rabble and did not really talk, as it was difficult with all the noise and commotion. Not even two minutes later, we arrived at a bus stop. I thought Hector would then leave, but instead, he took out a pack of cigarettes and offered me one.

"No thanks. I don't smoke."

He smiled, "A good thing, as they are bad for you." He took one out and lit it. He then enjoyed the moment of relaxation amongst the masses before continuing. "The bus stops right outside the embassy," he puffed out. "I will tell the driver to drop you there, and then, when you're finished, just wait at the bus stop across the road from where you get off."

"It's that simple?"

"That simple," he said. I loved talking to Hector, because he talked to me like his adult friend rather than a child. He was probably the most comfortable person for me to be around during my whole time in Istanbul. Buses came and went, and then with a jump, Hector threw his cigarette end on the street. "Here it is." He was waving frantically and shouting like a maniac in Turkish. He then winked at me and said, "You have to shout to be heard sometimes." As the bus came to a screeching halt, Hector looked at me again. "Do you have a 100 Lira note?"

"Yes."

"Give it to me." Without hesitation, I pulled out a 100 Lira note and gave it to him. The bus stopped and Hector jumped ahead of me and began to talk to the driver in Turkish. He then put the note in a machine instead of a ticket and the machine accepted it.

"I told him to drop you outside the embassy," he shouted above the noise of the engine. "You don't need a ticket when you come back, just put another 100 Lira note in the machine, and it'll be fine." Then he jumped off and waved at me.

"Thank you very much," I said in disbelief.

"Don't mention it," he smiled back. "Just remember me when you change money."

"I will," I said as I waved at him. I then made my way to the back of the bus and sat quietly next to the window and tried to take in the atmosphere of this world-famous city.

I really did try and look out of the window, and I probably did. However, I cannot remember anything that I saw. I was just nervous and scared. My heart was beating at three times its normal pace. I was trying to go through all the possibilities that could arise at the embassy. What if there were no Iranians at the embassy? What would I do then? How would I be able to communicate? It all was going to be a struggle. At no point did I think about not going, I just remember it being one of those things that you really didn't want to do, but there was no way round it. I knew that I just had to bite the bullet and give it a shot. Suddenly, the bus stopped, and I was still in my own little world. There was a shout, which caught my attention. It was the driver. He was waving at me to suggest that I should get off. I suddenly realized that I was there. I quickly got off the bus and waved at the driver as he drove off. The road was fairly busy, but not as busy at the market place. The embassy, as I used to think of it, was actually a consulate.

Huge, black towering gates stood in front of me. Two armed guards at each end of the gate stood motionless as I approached. A couple had just walked through the gates as I got off the bus. The famous Union Jack flew proudly at the gate tower. I checked my pockets for my passport one more time. I slowly approached the gates, but to my surprise nothing happened. The gates did not open. I looked at one of the guards, and he seemed to be completely ignoring me. So I turned my head and looked at the other guard. He was looking at me, but he said nothing. So I asked, "Can you let me in, please?"

They ignored me once again. I could not believe it. I went up to gates and began to pull on them in fury. Then one of the guards came over to me and effortlessly removed my hands from the gates. He said something to me, but I did not know what he was saying. So I looked at him again and said, "I need to go in," this time pointing at the building in the distance. "Please let me in."

Once again, he said something to me that I clearly did not understand. However, it was clear that he did not intend to let me in. Therefore, I got out my passport and started to wave it at them. "Please let me in," I screamed. "I am an Iranian citizen, and I want to apply for a visa."

I think my infuriation merely amused the two guards as they were laughing at me. I did not know what to do, and without even realizing it, I cried. I just stood there and cried in front of the two guards. Then I spoke to them in a sob, "Well, I am not leaving until you let me in."

Then I walked up to the gates and sat on the floor; there I held the gate bars and continued to sob. Then the guard came over to me and said something that must have been an order for me to move, as he was waving his hands to suggest a motion away from the gates. I decided not to budge and stayed still. Then the guard manhandled me and lifted me up in one easy scoop and put me down on the edge of the pavement away from the gate. Immediately, I rose to my feet and ran back to the gate and retook my previous position. To the guard's frustration, he had to repeat his previous move and put me back on the edge of the pavement. He was beginning to get angry, and his tone of voice was changing, but I was determined to hold my ground. This little standoff continued for at least another four or five times until I was back at the gate, and the guard knew that he had to regroup to come up with a better plan. His friend said something to him that made him go into the little gate tower. I saw him lift up a white phone and began to speak into it while looking at me.

I had tears rolling down my cheeks, and I was nervous, as I did not know if I was in trouble or not. This conversation took place over about one minute, but it seemed to go on for much longer than that as I waited for my judgement. The guard came out and looked at me. He said something to me in a lower tone of voice that resembled the tone he used on out first encounter. Once again, I had no idea what he was talking about, and so I sat still holding onto the bars. He then looked at me and smiled. He then waved me gently away as he continued to speak. Again, I stood my ground. The guard looked at his friend, and they both smiled at me. The guard came again and lifted me up; I thought the game was back on. However, as he lifted me up, he did not put me down, and the other guard opened the gate. I was not sure what was going on, and so I started to kick out. I was scared they were going to beat me. Then the guard who opened the gate left the gate and walked away from it as he shouted out directions to his friend that had me in his arms. Then the guard put me down and ran a few feet away from him. They were both waving me in, trying to indicate that I would be seen inside. However, I was unsure of them and watched them like a hawk as I walked through the gates. As soon as one of them made a slight move, it would make me jump. Yet as soon as I got through the gates, they shut it behind me and took their old positions by the sides of the gates.

Even though I kept checking behind me to see if I was being tricked or not, I could not help but be overwhelmed by the sheer size and beauty of this consulate. A drive from the gates led me to the main entrance of the consulate building, about four hundred feet away from the gates. On either side of the drive were awesome gardens that had been manicured to the minutest detail. The lawns were mowed to the exact millimeter, the traditional English Charles Austin roses were in prime condition, and the trees stood in strategic areas of the garden offering shade to the pants that needed them. To me, it looked like all the stories that I had heard previously about the West were true. This place was like a fairyland. I just remember being impressed. For the first time since I had arrived in Istanbul, I had hope. Maybe what my father was doing was right. Maybe England was the place that was going to be best for me. I thought England was going to be just like the consulate.

The door to the main building was an extravagantly large oak door with huge handles. It was halfway open, and I remember walking through it wondering if I was doing the right thing by going straight in. There was a small corridor with more guards and what seemed like an orchestrator at the end. They stood by another glass door. I was not sure what to do until one of the guards waved me toward him. I went to him slowly, and there he patted me down to see if I was carrying anything dangerous. Then the orchestrator pointed to a little machine that had small tickets coming out of it. I pulled one out and then looked at the man to see what I should do next. He waved and spoke, suggesting that I should sit down. Amongst his waving motions, he had pointed to a display with red numbers on it. I realized that when my number would be displayed would be the time that they would see me.

My first impression was that it was like a large post office with windows of clerks seeing to people. The waiting area was packed with people. The number being displayed was 78 and my number was 114. I knew that I had a long time to wait. I was sweating and breathing quite quickly. The first part of the problem had been dealt with. I had found the consulate, I had managed to get inside, but now I had a completely different problem. I was listening to the different conversations at the different counters. They were being conducted in either English or Turkish. I didn't know what to do. I could not understand anything that anyone was saying to me. The only thing that I had going for me was time. I had a long time to wait. Therefore, I leaned down in my seat and put my head in my hands. I tried to blank everything out and think. Numbers were coming and going, and yet nothing was happening. I wanted my parents to be with me so badly. I could not keep doing this. I thought this kind of luck had to run out soon. Maybe that day was going to be the day. However, the concept of disappointing my father was always the factor that kept me going.

Suddenly I heard "Is that little boy crying?" It was the voice of a beautiful lady. She was Iranian and dressed in beautiful black clothes. She was so sophisticated, and her eyes were so kind. She looked at me as if I were her own child. She was with her husband, I think. I looked up at her and forced a smile through my tears.

"Are you alone?" she asked me. She was speaking quite loudly as she was across the room from me. So I nodded my head slowly to tell her that I was alone. "Can I come and sit with you?" she asked gently. So again, I nodded my head to confirm that I wanted her to sit next to me. It was there and then that I realized that my biggest weakness was also my biggest strength. My age was a huge factor in Istanbul. It made me a novelty and people paid attention to me, whereas if I were an adult, they would not have done so.

The lady said something to her husband and very elegantly made her way over to me.

"Hello," she said, as she sat next to me.

"Hello," I said quietly. I was milking the situation now, but it was working, so why stop a winning formula?

"What's wrong, Sweetheart?" she asked genuinely concerned.

I looked at her with my teary eyes and then pathetically said, "I'm here alone to apply for a visa, and I don't speak Turkish or English." I watched her face drop as I told her, "I don't know what to do."

"You're here alone?" she asked.

"Yes."

"Where are your parents?" she asked, halfway curious and halfway angry.

"In Tehran."

"Why are you here alone?" she asked.

"They wouldn't let my mother out, and my father did not want me to go to war," I explained, "and now I don't know how to speak to those people," as I pointed toward the windows.

"Would you like me to help you?" she asked. She was still trying to get over the shock of me being alone in foreign country.

"What is your number?"

"Oh," she said as she checked her ticket in her hand, "103."

"But I'm much later than you," I said, showing her my number. "You'd have to wait an hour or so longer."

"It's okay," she said gently as she rubbed my back. "I'll wait with you and translate."

"No, you don't have to do that," I said. Of course, I did not mean it, but I was practicing the great art of a Persian tradition called *tarof.* There is no direct translation in English, but it roughly means when one insists on not accepting hospitality just to be polite.

"Don't be silly," she said. "It will be my pleasure. Just let me tell my husband."

She walked over to her husband as elegantly as she came over to me. She whispered the tale in his ear, and suddenly, the man started to look harder at me. I'm not sure what he thought about the whole situation, but I was getting the impression that he wanted no part in it. However, the lady seemed insistent that she was going to help me. I didn't blame the man. At that time, everyone had their own problems, and the unwritten rule was that you went about your business and did not involve yourself in other people's. The lady stayed with husband, and eventually, their number was called. They both went up together, and they seemed to stay there forever as they talked for a good twenty minutes. When their business was finished, the couple came away from the window, and the man walked straight out. I thought that the lady had changed her mind too, and my head sank down back into my hands again. Now I really was in a jam as to my knowledge. There were no other Iranians there, and I had very little time now. The number was only two or three away from mine. Suddenly, there was a tap on my shoulders. I looked up to see the lady again.

"What's wrong?" she said.

"I thought you forgot about me," I said.

"How could I forget such a handsome face," she said with a smile. I was blushing but happy. I was out of my jam again. "My husband had to go as he has some business to take care of, but I'll stay until all your interview is over."

"Thank you so much," I said politely. "It means a lot."

"Don't mention it."

We sat there in silence as we waited for the scared 114 to appear. Every so often, the lady would look at me and smile, and I would smile again. Then the number appeared, and as I stood up in delight, she stopped for a second and asked, "By the way, what is your name?"

"Abbas," I said, "Abbas Kazerooni."

"I just needed to know that for the man at your counter," she explained. We walked up to the counter where a man in his mid-forties sat behind the glass screen. He was bald with round spectacles. He had sharp features with small suspicious eyes. The lady explained that she was translating for me, as I spoke neither Turkish nor English. The man looked straight into my eyes without any expression. Even though the lady was translating, he always looked at me when he was talking to me.

"Why are your parents not here?" was his first question.

"Because they would not let them out of the country," I explained.

"The government, you mean?" the lady asked to make sure.

"Yes."

Once the man had heard what I said from the lady, he looked back at me and said,

"So why did your parents send you here alone?"

Through the same route I explained. "Because my father did not want me to die in the war and wanted me to have a good education. My cousin, Mehdi, is in England, and he has said that he will be my guardian once I am there. I want to go there to avoid the war and get a good education."

Once the man had heard what I had said, he took my passport and had a look at it. He then looked straight at me while talking fast in English. "Listen to me," he said in an authoritative manner, "this better be the truth, or you will never step a foot on English soil. Do not ever lie to us. This is a unique case, and we need to see the relevant paperwork. You have to go away and come back with the your parents' permission for you to go to the UK. You have to have your cousin's name, address, telephone number, occupation, state of residency, and his written permission that he is willing to be your guardian."

The lady kindly wrote down all the man's requests on a piece of paper and handed it to me. The man looked at me again and said, "One more thing. Why are you trying to escape from the war at this age?"

Immediately, I retorted, "Because in Iran the recruitment age has been lowered, and boys cannot leave the country after that age. If I stayed, children like me would be picked first."

"Why are you so different?"

"Because my father had links with the Shah and is antiestablishment." The man looked at me a weird way, and then nodded to confirm that he understood.

"Okay," he said, "go away, and come back with all the paperwork that I have asked for, not some, but all."

Once I understood what he had said, I smiled at him and decided to practice some of my limited English. "Thank you very much," I said in English. The man suddenly stopped being his serious self and saw the funny side of what I had just done and smiled at me. I am great believer that certain moments are deciding factors in whether people like you or not, and I believe that little moment made that man like me. This was a surprise, as I don't think he liked many people! I had not achieved a lot, but I was happy that I had got through the day and achieved everything that I had had to do. I walked out with the lady and walked down the drive.

"Thank you so much for what you have done for me," I said.

"It was my pleasure," she said, "You don't lose that list. Keep it safe and tell your father when you speak to him next."

"He's ringing me tonight," I said. "I'll tell him then."

When we got to the gates, the guards looked at me again. This time I was smiling, and I waved at them. They waved back to say goodbye. I think I made a few friends that day, even if some were harder to make than others! The lady turned to me and said, "Are you going to be okay getting to your hotel?" she inquired. "That is where you are staying right?"

"Yes, I'll be fine," I said. "My bus stops right across this street. Thank you."

"My pleasure," she said, as she paused to think. "Listen to me, Abbas. I don't know you, but I know that you are a very special boy. Just take care of yourself, and stay out of trouble."

"Okay."

With that, she gave me a hug and a kiss on my cheeks and walked away. I did not even know her name, and just like that, she left. I never did see her again, but once again, a small and brief acquaintance in my life made the world of difference to me.

Slowly but happily I crossed the road and waited for the bus. Sure enough, within minutes, it appeared from around the corner. I waved frantically trying to imitate Hector from earlier. The bus stopped, and I had my 100 Lira note ready to put inside the machine. Then I got onto the bus and took my seat. All I could think about was speaking to my father that night and hoped that maybe he would let me speak to my mother too. I knew that I had only two other problems for that day. One was trying to figure my way back to hotel from the market place and next was finding some good cheap food. Once again, I knew that I had to tackle one problem at a time. So far so good.

CHAPTER 7

Sure enough, the bus took me back to the market place where it had picked me up from. I stood amongst the masses trying to find my bearings. I was a little lost, but the only thing that stopped me from panicking was the fact that there was some familiarity to where I was. I decided that the best way back would be to retrace my steps from the gates of the market place. So I crossed the road and walked to the market place entrance. I then remembered that I had walked in a straight line along the main road for about ten minutes. I just hoped that I would recognize the side road that led to the hotel. I knew that it was not too far away, but the city was so vast and so easy to get lost in. In the morning, I had thought about remembering my path, but I was so worried keeping my passport and money safe that I had forgotten about the route. It was exactly the same as the morning; the masses didn't care about anyone else. It didn't matter who they barged out of the way, who they pushed, or who they scared; they just cared about getting to their destinations as fast as possible. It was a good introduction to city life. Thinking back on it, it was not too different from Tehran. The only difference was that I never walked about in the center of Tehran by myself. This is why this city always seemed so evil to me.

Slowly I walked through the crowds, the speed of everything and everybody seemed so quick to me. I was talking to myself, praying that I would soon see the road that I had to take. As ever, I walked with my hands in my pockets to protect my money and passport. Suddenly, I realized that there was a piece of paper in my pocket. I had written my to-do list on a piece of hotel paper. It had the address and telephone number on it. Even though this did not really help me, I knew that in the worst possible scenario I could go inside a shop and ask for someone to show me how to get there. This piece of news really relaxed me, which in turn eased my journey. The people did not seem so bad, and they didn't seem to be pushing past me anymore. I wasn't quite yet one of them, but I didn't seem so lost. I had accidentally carried that piece of paper on me, but it was a good lesson. From there on, I decided to carry the hotel details on me in case this ever happened again. In fact, I was angry at myself for not having thought about it before. This time I had got away with it, but I knew that I would not be so lucky every time. Due to my circumstances, I had to prepare for every eventuality. I was just lucky that the lesson that taught me this was not a disastrous one. As all these thoughts were running through my head as I suddenly saw a shop that I recognized as my landmark for the right turn into my side street. It was a small kebab shop. I remembered it because the stench at that time of the morning really shocked me. It was open for business at 8 a.m., and I was horrified that people would eat something like that at such a time. It just didn't seem right to me!

To my delight, I jogged down my side road. Immediately, there was a different ambiance to the road. It hit the main road that led to the market place. Yet here it was quieter, dirtier, the people were not so well dressed, and the buildings were ugly. I could not understand how two roads at such close proximity could be so different. In the morning, I had not paid too much attention to my surroundings as I was with the couple and I was talking to them. This was the first time I had seen and paid attention to my road in daylight. Once again, the stench of coal and garbage hit me. Even the smell was different on the roads. I did not understand how people could live in such a place. I did not feel unsafe, but it seemed so dirty. It suddenly dawned on me that I was one of these people. I was also living here. Why was I living here? The answer was simple; I had to. Then I realized that everyone else that lived there also had to.

I was so happy to be back at the hotel. I had only been there one night—back and I had that feeling of *I'm so happy to be home.* By no means did I consider this hotel as my home, but it was the best I had, and it was my safety blanket in this foreign land. I was surprised to see Mourat sat at reception again as his shift had finished at 12 p.m. and it was 5 p.m. He could not have had any sleep. He was showered and changed, but he looked very tired and far from happy.

"Hello Mourat," I said. "I thought you finish at 12."

"I was supposed to," he gloomily told me, "but I got let down again. One thing you'll find here is that I'm like the furniture here."

"I see," I chuckled aloud, "but aren't you tired?"

"You get used to it," he said as he took a drag of a cigarette. "Did you have a good day?"

"Yes, thank you."

I had purposely kept it short and to the point, but I think curiosity got the better of Mourat, and he needed to know if I had succeeded in doing what I had planned on doing. "Did you swap money?"

"Yup," I said in realization, "which reminds me, can I have my dollars back, please? I have the Lira for you."

Suddenly Mourat realized that he had messed up, as he had reminded me of getting my dollars back. "Oh. sure," he sighed. "Quite the clever clogs, aren't we?"

I laughed even though I couldn't tell if he was making fun of me or not. Either way, I was happy because I was being accused of being clever! Mourat opened the safe under the reception and got $50 out of what seemed like a pile of dollars. I was amazed that such a small hotel had so much money in it. I gave him my Lira, and he counted it to the last bill. He was surprised that I handed over the exactly right amount. He did not know what to say. He merely nodded and gave me back my fifty. I was about to go upstairs when I turned and looked outside. The sun was setting, and I could tell that it was going to be dark soon.

Once again, I turned toward Mourat. "Sorry," I said softly, "can I ask you one more question?"

"Sure."

"Where can I buy some food and water from?"

"Oh, there is a corner shop about four hundred feet to the right. Just walk straight and you won't miss it."

"Thank you." Mourat smiled at me as if he knew that I really was thankful.

"Don't mention it. It's cheap there, but the food is good."

I smiled again and turned and walked straight out. I did not want to leave any later than it already was. Besides, I was really hungry. I had actually forgotten all about food, because I had been so busy and worried throughout the day. I also realized that I had a headache. I needed to drink water, but I did not know that at the time. I knew that I was thirsty, but I didn't know that the two were linked. My head was pounding, I was thirsty, I was hungry, and yet I was happy with myself. I did not know that I had it in me to get through the day.

The street looked even more ominous than it did when I returned from the consulate. It was getting darker, and the buildings looked even gloomier than before. Mourat was right, the shop was only four hundred feet away, but it seemed like the longest four hundred feet in the world. It was a scary street, and if anything was to happen, it looked like there was nowhere to run. As I was thinking about that, a small alley appeared to my right. I could not see how deep the alley went, as it was very dark down there. It was the only escape route from the road, apart from either end. I always used to think about escaping from different situations. Usually I was aware, watching for people who might chase me for my money or passport. I knew that I could not continue to carry my dollars on me as I had been, but I did not know where I could put them. I certainly did not trust anyone yet, and it was always in the back of my mind. It always made me edgier than I already was and more paranoid than I had ever been in my life. Anyone that passed me on the street was a potential thief. It was a horrible state to be in, as it created stress and that made me depressed.

Eventually, I caught sight of a little shop on the corner of the main road, which intersected with mine. It looked like a cute shop, the only cute thing about my street. Apart from my hotel, it was the only building or shop that illuminated any light onto the street, and that immediately warmed me to it. As I drew nearer, I realized the state of my hunger more and more. I could smell all the little delicacies from afar. As I approached, I could smell the freshly made bread, the cheeses, the meats, and the vegetables. I knew that I had to save my money, as I did not know the length of my stay. As soon as I opened the door, I felt like a child in Santa's grotto. I wanted to buy everything, but once again, the wrath of my father was in the back of my mind. A sweet gentleman was behind the counter attending to his shelf stacking. He turned to me and smiled. I smiled back at him and continued to snoop around the shop. I went straight to the little bakery that he had and picked up the biggest loaf of bread. It then turned around and looked at the toasting machine that he had, and it smelt so good. I did not know how to communicate, so I merely groaned out, "Emmm . . . ," and then pointed to the meat.

"Iranian?"

"Yes," I said with surprise, "how much is that?"

"This meat," he said with a laugh, "is called Kavourma—1000 Lira for one sandwich."

"I see," I said. I was always thinking in terms of dollars, and that seemed expensive. "What about the yogurt?"

"Oh that, 150 Lira for tub." That sounded much better to me. It could last two days probably. So all I needed was the water, as you could not drink the tap water in Turkey. I picked up a big bottle and put it on the counter.

"That is all?"

"Thank you, yes," I said politely.

"Are you here on holiday?"

"Yes," I replied. I could not bother myself with explaining the details of my situation again, and I just wanted to get home and eat.

"How long?"

"Not sure."

"Oh I see," he said knowingly. It seemed like all the Turks were aware of what I was doing there. "So what is your name, Little Man?" I could not understand it, but everyone kept calling me Little Man. None of the people that had referred to me as that knew each other, and yet it all seemed like a conspiracy to me. I guess this was a coincidence, but my paranoia was getting the better of me. This question made me slightly jumpy, and I wanted to get out of the shop as soon as I could. I did not know why this was, as the man was very nice, and my instincts told me that this was a good man. However, this "Little Man" business was scaring me a little. I liked the name, but I had not told anyone about it, and yet three people randomly had named me so. Nevertheless, I decided to answer the man politely, as I knew that I would be visiting his shop frequently. "Abbas Ufundy." I had heard others call older men "Ufundy," which meant "sir" or "mister."

When I said that, the man laughed and chuckled. "I think I will like you, Abbas, but I think I will call you Little Man."

During our conversation, I had already paid the man. On his last remark, I turned toward the door to bolt when I remembered that I should be polite. "Thank you, Ufundy. I will see you again soon."

"Bye, Little Man."

All the way home, I was jogging, as it seemed like everyone was out there to get me. I was quite scared, even if the man had been really nice to me. At that particular time, I felt like the entire world was laughing at me, and this was one big joke. It was lonely there. I could not speak to anyone; I could not really ask for help from anyone, and everyone seemed to know things that I didn't. It just didn't seem fair. It was far too hard and very different from the life that I was used to. This was not quite the point in my life where I learned that life was not fair, but it was certainly my first realization of it. Once again, I had to play mind games with myself to keep my spirits up. I kept telling myself that it would be okay, as my father would be pleased with me when he rang later. I also knew that I had to keep myself busy, and so I started to think about budgeting for food. I knew that I had been good at buying only the things that I did. However, I knew that I could not keep this up, so I decided there and then to reward myself every Friday with a Kavourma sandwich. This would be something to look forward to during the week and would also help me keep my focus. At that age, concentration and focus were the hardest things to maintain. Luckily, I knew myself, and I knew that by rewarding myself I would keep to my budget the rest of the week. I had chosen Fridays; in Iran, Fridays are the resting days. This inner dialogue took place over the space of time that it took me to jog four hundred feet. One can imagine the stress that my mind was under at that time. I never stopped thinking. The thinking kept me alive and kept me going emotionally as well physically, but it also had its consequences emotionally too. That, along with the loneliness, fear, and paranoia paid its toll.

Eventually, I got back to the hotel, and with a wry smile, I walked past an unknowing Mourat. This was the first time I had returned to my room. I was scared that my things would not be there. The bed had been made with more damp sheets and the bathroom looked a little cleaner. It was as dirty as the previous night, but in better condition than I had left it in. I then slid open the cupboards and checked through my clothes. Then I went through my papers to find pictures of my family. This stopped me in my tracks. It was apparent that everything was intact. I was motionless looking at the pictures, especially of the ones of my mother. I missed her an unbearable amount, not that one can measure such things. I could not take the image of her in the airport out of my mind. There was nothing more upsetting to me than seeing my mother in that state. The image of her on her knees crying just would not leave me. I felt very guilty for obeying my father. I felt like I betrayed a sacred bond that we had together. I had let her down by not even hugging her or kissing her good bye. Now I could not even speak to her. I wished my father would allow me to speak to her that night.

I put the pictures down slowly in front of me so that I could look at them while I ate. I could just imagine Mamanjoon asking me if I wanted tea if I had been in Tehran. I opened up the bag to look at my bread and yogurt. First, I opened up the bottle of water and gulped down a third of it in one go. Then I looked at the bread and yogurt. I was determined that they would last me for that night and the following day. I very neatly measured half of the loaf with a small ruler and cut it in a half. Then I broke the first piece of bread off with my hands and dipped it into the yogurt. I remember that the first bite tasted so good. I was so hungry that anything would have tasted good. I thought to myself how only three months previously I would have put my nose up to such a measly offering. The speed at which things had changed was amazingly swift. I was living by myself, taking care of my own business, washing myself, and now feeding myself. This was my first meal, and as ever, the first was the hardest. I missed the little quarrels of my household. I missed our conversations at meal times, I even missed school, but most of all, I missed the security and safety that I had in Tehran. By the fifth mouthful, the blandness of my meal was showing. I still didn't care that much as I was still hungry, but my mother's cooking was badly missed.

When I had half of the yogurt and bread, I neatly put the top back on the pot and placed it by the window in order to keep it cool. Then I wrapped the bread up in the plastic bag that the shopkeeper had given to me and placed it on the bedside table. I took another few sips of water and placed the bottle next to the bread. Now what was I to do? It was not even 7:30 p.m., and I was bored. So I decided to venture into the lobby. I locked the door behind me, checked it, and then trotted downstairs. Mourat took his usual position in the lobby.

"Hi," I muttered. "How are you?"

"Tired!"

"You need to sleep."

"Thanks, Doctor, I'll remember that!" he moaned with a sense of sarcasm that I warmed to. I just chuckled back at him, showing my satisfaction at his humor. I think he got a little kick out of managing to entertain me. "There's a television room if you have nothing to do."

"There is?"

"Yeah," he smiled, "just go down the corridor there and turn left."

"Thanks," I hesitantly replied, "but I am waiting for a phone call."

"I'll get you. I know where you are."

"Oh, thanks, Mourat."

"Sure thing."

This was the first thing that sounded like fun since I had arrived in Istanbul. In Iran, there were only two stations, and they were mainly programmed with religious shows. It was a small thing, but it made me happy in the short term. I think Mourat realized how excited I was about it, as he also got some satisfaction from my delight. The corridor led to a small bar at the back of the hotel, which in turn led to the television lounge to the left of it. It was a small but nice room. There were a few Iranians sitting there, either drinking tea or beer. I took my place at the back of the room and settled down to watch whatever the crowd was watching. The first program that I ever saw was Knight Rider. Wow! What a show! It blew my mind. If all programs were like that, then I was going to have a good time. All the Iranians were talking about it and how famous it was in the West. It was badly dubbed into Turkish, but I didn't care. I could make out roughly what was going on, and the car was what excited me.

I was sat there for at least a few hours watching Turkish television. It was amazing. I had forgotten about everything. I understood none of it, but it was so amazing to me. I had never seen an advertisement before. I even loved them too. Suddenly, there was a little tap on my shoulder

"Hello, you." It was Assal. I was quite happy to see her, as everyone in the lounge had company apart from me. No one had said anything to me, and I had kept to myself. It was nice to see that I was recognized by someone, even though she was just an acquaintance.

"Hello, Assal. Nice to see you again."

"You're such a sweet little boy," she said with a gentle look. She then stroked my cheek, which made me blush a little. "Your mother must have taught you good manners."

"Yes, she did," I said quietly, as I tried to avoid any attention.

"So how did it go today, Sweetheart?"

"Oh, good, thanks," I said excitedly. "I swapped fifty for a really good rate and then went to the embassy." I was really excited that I achieved all this, so I offered a bit more information than I should have. "They told me what papers I needed. My father is calling tonight, so I'll tell him what to send me."

"You are a clever boy, aren't you?" Thinking back on it, I can't figure out if comments like that were genuine or patronizing, but at the time, I certainly took them as compliments, as I needed all the encouragement in the world.

"Thank you."

"So what was your real good rate then?" a deep voice asked from the other side. I had not noticed him, but Ali had crept in and listened to some of the conversation. I didn't want to reply, but I was somewhat cornered in. I guessed that I should tell the truth, and I would find out if I had been swindled.

"1000 Lira a dollar."

"1000?" Assal screamed.

"There's no way," Ali said with an arrogant smile. "He's lying." He then walked off not even bothering with what I had to say.

"I didn't lie, Assal," I said angrily. "I don't lie. I got a 1000."

"I believe you, Sweetheart."

"Why doesn't he like me?" I asked sadly. "What have I done to offend him?"

"Nothing, my darling," she muttered in an embarrassed manner. "He doesn't like anyone."

"Surely he likes you," I said as a matter of fact. She looked at me in a way to suggest the opposite, but smiled through her sadness.

"Yes, Sweetheart." She was not fooling anyone; it was obvious that she was unhappy. It was strange that she was confiding this to a complete stranger, and what's more, a child. "Do you want a glass of tea?"

"Oh, no thank you," I said. I did not want to start a tab and order tea like everyone else. My budget was very important to me, and I knew I could not afford such luxuries.

"It's okay, Sweetheart. I'll get it for you."

"It's okay, Assal. You don't have to do that," I said. "I have money."

"I know you do, but I want to treat you." I really didn't want tea, because I did not want her to buy it for me, and I didn't want to buy it for me either, so I thought I would decline her offer one more time.

"Really, it's okay. Thank you."

"I insist," she said stubbornly.

"Okay then," I replied, "thank you very much."

"I'll be right back." I watched her go to the bar and order the teas. On her way, she said hello to a few Iranians on her way. They got to talking, but the level of her voice suddenly dropped by at least half. I pretended not to be listening, but I could hear some of what she was saying. She was telling them that I was alone and how much of a nice boy I was. I could hear all the "Ahhhs" and "Bless hims" from where I was sitting. I was blushing, but I was still pretending to watch television. I could see from the corner of my eye that everyone was turning to have a good look at me, one by one. I could sense that the women amongst them were more drawn to me. Perhaps it was their motherly instincts, but on the whole, the men were not as interested in my affairs.

About ten minutes later, Assal arrived back with the tea. She put it down in front of me and looked at me. "Enjoy, Abbas," she said with tears in her eyes. He tone of voice was extremely melancholic and so low that only I could hear what she was saying. "You take real good care of yourself, you hear me?"

"Yeah, I will," I said in a state of shock. She was making me feel nervous. I did not understand why she was speaking to me like this.

"You do that; Istanbul can be a nasty place."

"Okay." Then she leaned down and kissed me on the cheek and left. Honestly, I could have done without her last comment. I was scared enough without her help. However, I was frightened for her too. Something was not right, but I did not know what. As it turned out, that was the last time I ever saw her or Ali. I found out later that they fled Istanbul because Ali was wanted by some gangsters for taking their money for promised forged visas. Nevertheless, he had let them down, and they were after him. Someone told me the people after him were not the friendliest in Istanbul. I only really understand it now, but it was enough to scare me at the time, because I thought they might come after me because I had talked to him a few times!

I had completely forgotten about my father calling. I was aware of the Iranian population still coming in and out of the lounge to get a good look at me, but I decided to ignore that.

Around 10:30 p.m. Mourat ran into the lounge. "Abbas, phone call." It was short, sharp, and to the point. It brought me out of my zone, and I jumped to my feet and ran toward the cubicles after Mourat. As I ran, I reached inside my pockets for the piece of paper that had written on the papers that I needed. As I entered the reception area, Mourat held up his index finger suggesting cubicle one. I ran into it and picked the phone up.

I guess I was hoping, when I shouted, "Maman?"

"No, it's me," my father said.

"Oh, hi, Baba. Can I speak to Maman?"

"No, Abs, she's ill at the moment. Maybe tomorrow if she's feeling better." I could tell by his tone of voice that he was lying, but I did not carry on with this topic as I knew that I would be disappointed.

"Okay," I said despondently. There was a pause as my father gathered his thoughts. I don't think that he expected that in the first thirty seconds of the conversation. I didn't speak, because I just wanted to speak to my mother, and he was not allowing me to do so.

"So how are you?" he asked.

"Good thanks," I groaned, "and you?"

"Oh, we're all fine, apart from your mother who has the flu or something."

"Tell her I said hi."

"I will," he replied as he got his thoughts together again. "So what happened today?"

"Sorry?" I was still in my own little world thinking about my mother.

"The embassy and the money swap," he snapped. "Come on Abs; get with it."

I could not believe he was shouting at me. I had tears rolling down my cheeks, but I was determined not to let him know.

"Sorry, Baba," I said quietly, "I went to the market this morning, and then checked all the money dealers, and I got the best price in town. No one got the same price as me."

"Which was?"

"1000 Lira a dollar."

"Don't lie to me, Abs," he said almost disappointed. "Tell me the truth."

"I am! I got 1000. Why does everyone think I am lying? I never lie."

"It's okay, Abs," as he paused. "Did you really get 1000?"

"Yes," I snapped. "I only swapped $50 because the rate changes every day, like you said."

"Good lad," he said, "that is amazing. I don't think I could have done any better myself."

"Probably not, nobody did today." There was a silence as he thought about shouting at me for my arrogance and insolence, but honestly I didn't care, as I felt unappreciated and unloved at that particular time. Maybe he did not realize how difficult this was for me. He decided to ignore it.

"And the embassy?"

"I went there by bus, and I spoke to the man there."

"You did?"

"Yeah," I went on, "he told me that I need the your permission for me to go to the UK, Mehdi's full name, address, telephone number, occupation, state of residency, and his written permission that he is willing to be my guardian."

"He told you all that?"

"Yeah."

"And you remembered it all?"

"Yes, but I also wrote it down so that I wouldn't forget."

"I see," he said in shock, "you did this all by yourself?"

"No," I said as a matter of fact, "I can't speak English or Turkish, and so I asked for help from an Iranian lady, and she agreed to translate." There was a huge pause as he thought to himself. He could not understand how I had accomplished all this. Well, at least that is what it sounded like, or that is what I liked to think.

"Well done." I decided not to thank him, as I was angry at him. After all that, I got a "Well done?"

"So how are you?" he went on.

"Good," I said, "the hotel is great; the area is really nice in the day and . . ."

"You're not spending too much are you?" I remember feeling so sad and angry at the same time. I'm not sure how much belief he actually had in me, and I was going out of my way to make him proud. I was depressed, I was scared, I was hungry, I was paranoid, and it seemed like he did not understand any of this. For such a wise man, he was somewhat disillusioned.

"No, Baba, I only bought my bus tickets, paid for my hotel, got my dollars back, and for food, I bought a loaf of bread, pot of yogurt, and a bottle of water."

"That's it?"

"I promise."

"Okay," as he paused again, "you're a good lad. Just stay in the hotel, don't leave unless you have to, and certainly don't leave at night. Wait there, and I will send you the papers as quickly as I can. I will call you either tomorrow night or the day after."

"The day after tomorrow?"

"Yes, I can't call you everyday, Abs. It's very expensive."

"Yeah," I moaned, trying hard not to show my disappointment.

"I will do my best, Abs," he said desperately. "The papers will be with you soon."

"How soon?"

"About 7 to 10 days I should think."

"How long?" Yet another pause—tension filled the line.

"I know, Abs. You're just going to have to be strong for me, okay?"

"I will."

"Okay, Son. You take care, and I'll call you as soon as I can."

"Bye."

The phone clicked on me again; I couldn't believe it. I wished he had not called at all. Once again, I had to dry me tears before leaving the booth, as I could not have everyone seeing me in this state. That was certainly a low point in Istanbul. I thought my father would be proud of me. I guessed that he was, but I wished that he had said it. I really needed a boost but that was definitely it. I already felt lonely and the people that had always made me feel wanted were letting me down. My mother would have not talked to me in that way but I was not allowed to talk to her again. My father had not been the warmest person on that occasion. It must have been hard for them, too, but at least they had each other.

CHAPTER 8

I returned to the television lounge and slid into the back row of seats where I could hide my melancholy in the darkness. I watched television, and it brought me some pleasure, but not like before my phone call. My mind was still on the conversation that I had with my father. I was certain that he would be pleased with what I had done, but it did not come across that way. I would have been so pleased with a mere "I'm proud of you." At this point, I thought that it could not get any worse. I just wanted to return home, but I was now sure that my father would have never been the same with me again. He had always set high standards, which I liked. However, this was a very hard regime for me, and I was not sure if I could match his expectations this time. I had not been brought up or trained for this type of life. I had by no means come from a very privileged background in an economic sense, but emotionally, I had been spoiled. I had to learn to adjust, but I did not know how. Change was not something that I was used to.

I stayed in the lounge until about 2 a.m. when everyone else had gone to bed. I was watching late night television and avoiding going to bed because so far that had been the hardest thing—falling asleep in that hotel room. I hated the lonely and vulnerable feeling that used to go through my spine. Every noise and every shadow seemed like a potential danger to me. That, along with the damp sheets and the cockroaches, was a little boy's nightmare. I did not even know what I was watching, but I was adamant about not moving. As I was thinking about the inevitable move, I noticed a smiling Mourat stood at the door.

"Not tired?"

"No," I lied.

"You like this?" as he pointed to the television. It looked like a documentary on lorry drivers in Turkey! So I shrugged my shoulders to say that I did not mind.

"I'm practicing to be a receptionist," I commented with a straight face. Mourat was shocked at the level of my dry humor, but forced a smile from the side of his mouth. I could see that he was entertained by

my comment. He nodded at me and slid back to his post. Even though the television was not loud and Mourat had not asked me to leave the lounge, I felt like I should against my will. Therefore, I slowly got up and walked toward the television and turned it off. With shuffling feet, I walked to the bottom of the stairs when I thought I would say good night to Mourat. It was yet another excuse to put off the move upstairs. Mourat stood by the lobby door smoking a cigarette. At the noise of my shuffling, he turned to see who it was.

"Going to bed?"

"Yup," I said as a matter fact. "I thought I would come and say good night first."

"Oh," he said with surprise, "thank you. Good night to you too."

"I turned the TV off."

"Thanks, I could have done that."

"I know." There was a pause as I was desperately trying to think of something to say in order to stay downstairs. "Are you on all night?"

"Well, until 5a.m. supposedly," he sighed, "but we'll see if that actually happens or not." I did not have anything else to say, so I was about to turn away when I heard, "What are your plans for tomorrow?"

"Nothing."

"You have no business to take care of?" he inquired.

"No, I am waiting for some paperwork so . . ."

"I know," he smiled, "you have to kill time without spending money." I just nodded. He obviously knew what was going on. I think he must have seen people doing this kind of thing everyday for at least the last three years before I had arrived.

"It's okay," he said. "We have things to do to kill time here."

"You do?"

"Yes, we do," he said with a knowing smile. I was quite excited at the prospect of having something to do, as I knew that I would get bored, but I was curious as what it actually was.

"Does it cost anything?"

"Free!"

"Well, what is it?"

"That, my friend, you have to wait until tomorrow for." He could

see that my mood was slightly changed, and he got a kick out of the fact that it was him who did it.

"Good night, Mourat," I said with a smile. I liked him more and more as he always seemed to care in his casual way.

"Good night Abbas."

I was about to walk off when curiosity got the better of me. "Mourat?"

"Yes?"

There was a little pause as I thought about what I was going to ask and if the answer was going to make me feel better or not. I decided to go ahead with it anyway. "Have any children my age stayed here before?" I asked and then realized that the question was not complete. "Alone, I mean."

Mourat looked at me knowingly and said, "No."

"Okay," I said softly, "thank you." I don't know what I thought his question would achieve, but it had two sides to it. It made feel special because I was the first, and of course, that made me proud. On the turn side, it made me feel scared because I did not know if I was a good enough person to get through what was ahead.

So I strolled upstairs and through the dark corridor to my hotel room door. I held my breath and got myself together. My mother had always told me that doing something for the first time was the hardest, and then it would get easier. I was waiting for this part of the day to get easier, but it seemed as hard as the first night. However, in the back of my mind, I knew that I had got through the first night. Slowly, I opened the door and peeped my head inside. Everything was as I had left it. The smell of damp and the breeze coming from the gap in the window immediately hit me. The atmosphere was always different in the room. One would think that the hotel room would be the place of solace, but to begin with, it was far from that and merely a sleeping station. I entered and routinely locked the door behind me. I certainly didn't feel like taking a shower, and so I was safe from that, but I still had to motivate myself to get into bed.

I sat on the bed and just listened. I could hear those little noises that I had heard the night before. Every person that wandered past on the street below my window was heard by me. I crept toward the edge of the room and swiftly closed the curtains so that no one could see me.

Following that, I got my photographs and held them in my hands, and then placed them on the second pillow next to me. Before settling down, I knew that I had to go and brush my teeth. So without fuss I walked into the bathroom and turned on the lights. The cockroaches were dancing in the corners as ever. I tried hard to keep them out of my mind, but they gave me the creeps. I couldn't help but always look around my feet to make sure they were nowhere near me. I brushed and brushed and remembered my mother teaching me how to go through the motions of daily dental hygiene. It brought a little smile to my face thinking how I always used to do everything I could to avoid these daily routines. Because there was no one to tease, I would them by myself.

Having returned to the main room, I stripped and put on my pajamas once again. I pulled back the sheets to get in, and then I stopped to look at the light switch. For the second night running, I could not bring myself to turn the lights off. I don't know what difference it made, but it made me feel a bit easier at the time. So I continued with the motion of turning back the sheets to get in. I could feel that the sheets were damp again, and I hated it so much. I hated not having that warm and safe feeling that my bed gave me back home. Momentarily, I closed my eyes and got into the bed pretending it was warm, but never mind how hard I tried, I could not keep out the cold. The damp on that particular night went through my cotton pajamas so that I felt it on my skin. I saw no use in wearing the pajamas, and so I stripped to my pants. I lay there looking at my mother trying hard not to shiver. It was cold, and the draft was coming in harder than the previous night. I couldn't put on more clothes, because they would just get damp and make me colder. Once again, tears began to flow.

I didn't mind the hardship so much. It was the loneliness again. I could not look at the picture of my father that night. Maybe I was still sad about our conversation previously, but I wasn't looking to him for help. I held my mother's picture, and then I looked above me as if to God. I had never been brought up to be religious, and neither of my parents ever prayed. Mamanjoon always prayed; in fact, she prayed so much that it must have covered our portions too! However, this was the first real time that I remember looking to God and actually asking Him for assistance. I didn't just pray, but I whispered out dialogue as if He were there in person. I cannot remember what I actually said to Him, but

it was on the lines of:

"God, I don't know why this has happened to me or why I am being punished. If I have done anything wrong, I'm really sorry. I promise to be a good boy from now on. If I have to be punished and cannot return home, then so be it, but please let Maman come soon. This is really hard for me, and I'm not sure how long I can do this for. If I must be punished alone, then please help me get through it, as I can't do this alone. Thank you."

As I spoke those words, tears rolled freely onto the already damp sheets. I could not sleep once again. I felt tired, and the day had taken its toll on me, but my thoughts were everywhere. How long was I really going to have to wait? Was my father angry with me, or was he disappointed with me? When would I be able to see my mother again, or more to the point, when would I be able to speak to her again? What was I going to do while waiting for my papers? I always needed to be stimulated, or I got bored very easily, but I was aware of that problem. I also knew that if I were not busy, I would try to eat, and I could not financially afford to that. I did not wish to upset my father any further, and this was certainly not an option. I kept going back over the conversation. I could not see why he was upset like that. I thought I excelled and deserved some praise as one does when they are seven years old, but not according to my father. He had high standards, and I had obviously not met them on that occasion. I just remember that I cried so much that I was slightly dizzy looking through starlike tears at the light that was on. That is the last thing I remembered as I cried myself to sleep.

The next morning I woke up very early again. I had a quick peep outside the window, and it was not quite day yet. I knew that I had lots of time to waste, and so I went back to bed and managed to get another two hours of intermittent sleep. I kept jumping out of dreams at the slightest of noises, which came from all directions. I knew that I could no longer sleep in, and so I grudgingly rose from my bed. My skin was red and raw. I was cold, and it was obvious that it was because the sheets had been damp. I dared not say anything yet, as I was too scared to rock the boat. What would happen if I had to swap hotels? My father was sending papers, and I might not receive them. In addition, I did not want to go through the trauma of having to find another hotel. I might not be lucky again to find another Ahmed.

The shower was not swift on that day. I turned on the shower and the trickle was warmer, and it felt so good against my skin, which was freezing cold. I washed myself, but I did not want to move away from the heat of the water, and so I stood there motionless, underneath the lame force of the water. I stood there for so long that I chose to sit on the bathroom floor. I was anally retentive about hygiene, and so when I eventually did get up, I washed my rear for the second time, as I did not trust that floor. I dried myself and very carefully chose my clothing for the day. I knew that I was not going anywhere, so I wore my jeans with a T-shirt and an old sweater. I took my money and passport from under my pillow and put them in my jeans pocket. I was about to open the door when I caught a quick glance of the bread. It was very tempting, but I decided to have my meal at the end of the day to reward myself for getting through it. I opened the door and walked through it with a sense of satisfaction because I had managed to get through yet another night.

Maybe the next night will be easier, I thought. I would have to wait and see what happened. Something I had learned was that I could not predict what was going to happen. However, I learned that planning and going through all different scenarios did have a plus side. However, the thinking really made me tired and stressed, which depressed me. Thinking back on it, the first thought of the day was what to do with my money, the second was whether I should eat then or later, and the third was wondering if my father was still angry with me. They may seem inconsequential now, but to a seven-year-old boy, these are stressing subjects. I walked out of the room and carefully locked the door behind me. As I did, a large man with a moustache was walking up the stairs,

"Morning," he said in Farsi. He smiled at me and seemed quite pleased to see me. I recognized him as one of the men in the lounge the previous night, and he knew who I was.

So I smiled back and kept my head low, and I responded, "Good morning, sir."

He smiled once again and walked off another flight of stairs. I smiled to myself and walked slowly downstairs. In my traditional way, I walked into the lobby. I was expecting a new receptionist, but sure enough, Mourat was there. He smiled at me knowingly.

"I thought you were . . ."

"So did I," he said with a sigh, "so did I."

"Do you ever sleep?"

"It appears not," he yawned, "the . . ." He proceed to call him a name. As soon as he said it, he put his hand in front of his mouth. "I'm sorry."

"It's okay," I said laughing at him. "I know all the bad words anyway."

He laughed aloud and then continued, "Well, yeah, this is the fourth time this new guy let me down," he snapped, "but when you have your own business, you have to make sacrifices."

"That's what my father says."

"He's a wise man," he said.

"So is this hotel yours?" I asked quietly.

"Half mine."

"Whose is the other half?"

"You ask a lot of questions, Little Man!" he said with a smile.

"So do you," I retorted without thinking. Fortunately, Mourat saw the funny side to my remark.

"Yes, you're right," he said, "that I do." He sat up in his chair and lit a cigarette.

"The other half of the hotel belongs to a silent partner." He saw that I was looking at him strangely. "That means that he does not work here. As in silent, I make all the decisions."

"So you are the boss?"

"Ah-huh!"

"Cool."

Mourat chuckled as he puffed on his cigarette, "Not so cool when you don't sleep!" he said. "So what are you going to do with yourself today?"

"I'm not sure really . . ." It was clear that I was out of ideas, because I had stopped mid-sentence.

"Why don't you write another letter to your parents?"

"Yeah, I could do that," I frowned. "Oh, by the way, did you . . ."

"Yes, I sent it with the post yesterday!" He anticipated my question, and to his credit, he guessed right.

"Thank you."

"My pleasure," he said with a friendly smile. "If you want any more paper and a pen, just help yourself here." He handed me some paper, a pen, and a few envelopes.

"Thank you, Mourat," I said softly. "How much do I owe you for the stamp yesterday?"

"Oh, nothing," he said with a wave of a hand. "Just don't tell anyone else, that's all. This is a deal only for my favorite customers!"

I smiled at him and touched my nose. "Our little secret," I said."Thank you very much."

"Thanks for what?"

"Thanks for . . . ahhhh!" as the penny dropped!

Mourat gave me a little wink and walked off to the kitchen, probably to make himself a glass of tea. I walked over to the sofas next to the phone booths and began to write my second letter to my mother. This letter was definitely going to be addressed to my father. I had a lot of hostility toward him at that point. I think that I felt that he had been unfair with me. Having said that, children tend to feel as if they have been treated harshly! My second letter went as follows:

Dear Maman,

How are you? I am doing very well. As I am sure you know, yesterday I went to the city to swap some money. I went inside a very big market with all sorts of dealers. They are really pushy! They don't like it when you tell them "No!" Anyway I found a really good man who gave me the best rate in Istanbul. I got 1000 Lira for as dollar. Baba thought I was lying, but I promise that I wasn't. You know that I don't lie, Maman. The city is really beautiful with really big buildings everywhere. There is this huge mosque, which you can see from everywhere. I WISH YOU WERE HERE TOO.

After the money swap, I went to the British Consulate. I got the bus there! It was fun and it was cheap. Here they let you just put the money in a machine, you don't even need a ticket! I had to wait a long time at the consulate, but it was okay. I was really scared at first, but this lady helped me. She was really nice. Anyway, the man told me to go away and get all these papers. I can't remember what they are as the list is upstairs in my room, but I'm sure that Baba has told you what I need. So here I am, waiting to receive them. The television channels are so much better than they are at home. My favorite program is called Knight Rider. It is so cool! However, I have only seen programs that were on last night. Maybe next time I will have a different favorite!

You would be proud of me as I am having at least one shower a day and brushing my teeth twice a day like you taught me. I am also only eating once a day like Baba told me to. I get hungry sometimes, but if I keep myself busy, I forget.

I really hope to speak to you soon, Maman, as I miss you so very much.

I love you,
Your son, Abbas
P.S. Please don't tell Baba that I was scared at the consulate.

I sealed the letter inside the envelope and addressed it. Then I left it in exactly the same place that I had left my last letter. Mourat was somewhere else at that point in time. It was mid-morning, and I had written my letter. I did not know what to do with myself, and so I thought the television room was worth a try. I went through to the bar and then to the lounge to find two women cleaning it. So that idea was a no go for at least another hour. I returned to the lobby to find Mourat with yet another tea, looking cross.

"What's wrong?" I asked.

"Have you seen that lady Assal and her husband?"

"Not since last night," I said, "why?"

"They have left without paying."

"How?" I asked. "You take money in advance."

"Not to old customers."

"Oh," I said disappointedly. "I see."

"What? Don't look at me like that. If you stay more than four weeks, you can pay at the end of every week because we have built trust."

"I thought we already had."

"Yes, we have," he said, "but it's not like that with everyone else is it?"

"I guess not."

"So with them, well they stayed six weeks, and then they asked for credit. I gave it to them, because they had paid before that."

"So how did they get away?" I think the husband left first and waited on the street while the woman threw their bags out of the window in the middle of the night," he explained. "Then I saw her leave at around 2 a.m."

"I'm sorry," I said.

"So am I," he sighed. "It's not the first time, and it won't be the last time. Oh, by the way, don't you tell anyone about the credit thing I told you about."

"I won't," I said with a smile. I touched my nose in the manner that I had done when we had decided to keep the secret of the stamps between ourselves.

"Good," he said, "then after next week, you can pay at the end of every week. Okay?"

"For real?" I asked.

"Yeah," he said, "but if anyone finds out about this, our deal is off."

"I promise." He offered his hand to show that this was a gentleman's deal. I reached out and shook his hand as firmly as my little hands allowed me to.

"So what are you planning to do with the rest of your day, Little Man?"

I shrugged my shoulders to show my lack of ideas.

"Okay," he said with a devilish smile. "I know what I can teach you to do."

"What?"

"Patience," he said, "all good things to those who wait." He returned to his desk and sat on his chair and picked up some papers. "Once I've got through these, I'll come and show you."

"Thank you." He smiled at me and then went into his work zone as he worked through his way through the papers. I could have gone and done something, but I had nothing to do. So I sat silently on my sofa and watched him do what he was doing. He had such large bags around his eyes. He was young, but the work had aged him somewhat. I could tell he was a good man, but he always looked troubled, even when he looked happy. Something in his eyes told me that, but I never found out what it was. He was very professional and discreet. Unless he had to, he kept himself to himself, and throughout my stay at his hotel, I was the only guest he conversed with on a regular basis. A few people came and went through the lobby. Two guys in particular caught my attention as they were young and badly dressed. Their clothes were ripped, their hair was messy, and they were obviously on something. I remember that Mourat raised his head as they left the hotel. I could see his look of disapproval as he stared at them until they left.

He then looked at me and said, "They're not going to be staying here tonight."

The way he said that was as a matter of fact. He genuinely meant it. I never did see how he evicted them, but that moment was an important one for me. This was because Mourat obviously saw what I saw and did not want that kind of clientele in his hotel. It was by no means the Hilton, but he had standards. It still did not feel like home, but it made feel that little bit easier.

It must have been a good hour until Mourat finished with his business. At no point did I make a noise or say anything to him. I sat silently and watched patiently, as he had asked. True to his word, once he had finished, he slowly put the papers to one side and rose from behind the desk with a big smile.

"So then, Little Man, do you have any idea what I am about to teach you?"

"No," I said. I really had no idea and could not wait until he told me.

"Okay," he said with yet another yawn. "What we are about to do needs tea. You cannot participate in this activity without a glass of tea."

"Oh," I said, "do I have to have one?"

"You don't have to have one," he said with a smile, "but if you want to play like a real Turk, then you have to."

"I see." I wanted tea, but I did not want to spend my money.

It was obvious to Mourat, and he gently smiled at me. "It's okay," he said. You're playing with the boss, remember, which makes the tea free."

"Oh," I said with joy, "are you sure?"

"Okay then—two glasses of tea coming up." He went to go into the kitchen, and then he came back in quickly and looked at me. "By the way," he noted, "this free tea . . ."

"I know. Don't tell anyone." I touched my nose again to Mourat's pleasure. He nodded with a look of approval.

"You're learning fast."

I watched him go out and then came back with two glasses of tea and some sugar cubes. He also had a large board, which I immediately recognized. He had a backgammon board with him. I had seen my father play with his friends in Iran, and I had always wanted to know how to play. I was extremely excited. Mourat sat down and opened the board.

"Right then, I'm about to make you into a real Turk." I did not say anything, as in Iran they made fun of Turks, and I knew what my father would have said to that remark. However, from what I had experienced, they had been nothing short of clever and hospitable.

Mourat spent the first thirty minutes teaching me how to play and the main rules. It was apparent to him that I was picking the game up very quickly, and so he decided to teach me the subtle intricacies of the game. I don't think he was expecting to take his tuition that far in the first two hours. We then decided to play a game, and in Istanbul, a game was usually the best out of five. In my first competitive game against an experienced player, I lost three games to two. Mourat promised that he was playing his best and was very impressed with my game. It was apparent to him that I had never played the game before due to the learning process prior to that. After the game, Mourat stood up and shook my hand.

"Little Man, we'll make a Turk out of you yet." I don't know what his obsession about making me into a Turk was really about, but I took it as a compliment.

"Thank you."

"Right, you can practice here if you want, as I have to get some sleep," he said, "but later on tonight, I'll give you another game if you want."

"Yeah," I said excitedly.

"I'll see you later then."

"Sure, but Mourat?"

"Yeah?"

"Who's gonna look after the reception?"

"No one," he said, "but I have to sleep. If anyone comes in, tell them we have no room."

"Okay."

"I'm going to be sleeping in the last available room." With that, he walked straight upstairs. Sure enough, no one was at reception. I stayed put and set the board up for a game against myself. I was extremely happy as I had learned to play a very traditional Middle Eastern game, and I was good at it. I cannot remember what happened, but time just flew. Happily, I played against myself for four hours without even noting the time. I was learning how to throw the dice, I was teaching myself new techniques, and I was happy about it. I don't know what I would have done if Mourat had not been there that day, but I was sure glad that he had.

Mourat appeared after four hours looking a little fresher. He had obviously had a shower, but he still looked tired.

"You only slept four hours!"

"I know," he said with a smile.

"Is that enough?"

"No, but it's four more hours than yesterday." He seemed to have a point, so I took the subject no further.

"How about you? What have you done?"

"I have played backgammon with myself."

"What? Since I left?"

"Yeah," I said, "and I helped myself to tea. Hope that's okay!" Suddenly, Mourat looked at me seriously, before realizing that I was joking.

"You're a live wire, Little Man," he said chuckling. "That's for sure." I just laughed at him.

"Talking of tea, can you get me a glass from the kitchen?"

"Who me?"

"Yeah, you," he said sitting down on a sofa next to me. "It's all right; you can get one for yourself too."

"I can?"

"Yeah, the pot is on the stove, and the glasses and sugar are next to the fridge."

"Okay."

I was about to run to my task when he called out to me again. "And when you get back, we'll see how good you really are at this game."

"You're on."

I ran to the kitchen and opened the door. I had never been in this room before. It was quite frankly disgusting. If a health and safety law had existed and it was policed, this hotel would have never survived more than a day. It was only a small kitchen, with rust, mold, and dust monopolizing all surfaces including walls. The glasses looked clean, but I washed two glasses under the tap anyway. The pot was there as he had said. I did not understand how it was hot. In all this time, I had forgotten to take note of the other employees of the hotel. There was a permanent barman and general handyman. There were a few part-time cleaners and a random guy whose job is an anomaly to me to this day. So I poured two glasses of tea, got some sugar cubes, and walked out to find Mourat sitting on the sofa with the backgammon board in front of him, ready to commence battle. Excitedly, I sat opposite him and away we went. Once again, it was an intense game, and I could see that Mourat was really trying. However, on this occasion, I beat him three games to one.

We did not really speak as we played, but once we were finished, Mourat looked up at me. His only words were "You make a good glass of tea."

This made me laugh, as it was completely unrelated to our game, and it seemed a long time ago since I had fetched the tea. Mourat did not comment on my game, but he did not really need to. I was quite happy with my efforts and knew that I was good at it. It was early evening now, and I had been playing backgammon for a fair few hours. I decided to take a break and go and watch some television. I still had not eaten, but I was saving it as long as I could. Mourat reclaimed his throne at reception, and I walked into the television lounge. I was the only person there. I turned it on, and like a robot, I took a seat and watched whatever the channels had to offer. Like a true vegetable, I sat there and observed for what seemed like a few hours. A few people came in and out, but nothing significant took place. Suddenly, there was a little tap on my shoulder from the barman. He was no longer in his waistcoat and looked like he had finished his shift.

His Farsi was not that great, but he did manage to say, "One minute, come with me, please?"

"Where?" I asked him.

"Just here," as he pointed to reception area. "Please, Mourat explain."

"Okay."

With slight hesitation, I got up from my seat and walked behind the barman. He was a funny fellow. He was very short and slightly overweight. His legs looked like they were arched, and he walked in a funny manner. In one's imagination, an eccentric character worked in such hotels all over the world. Here this barman was keeping up the stereotype in Istanbul. As I entered the lobby, I saw Mourat with a guy whom I had never seen before. He seemed very close with Mourat as they laughed together. He was dressed in a good suit and tie. He looked very smooth with a very neatly trimmed moustache, and his jet black hair was brushed back with some type of gel. It was a little too smooth for my liking.

"Ah," said Mourat like a host, "this is the little man I was talking about."

"Hello," said the man in perfect Farsi. "My name is Ali."

"Hello, I'm Abbas." We shook hands, but I was still not sure what this all had to do with me.

"I understand you only recently learned to play backgammon."

"Yes, today in fact."

"So it *was* today then," as he smiled at Mourat. "Did you tell him to say that?"

"I promise," Mourat replied with a smile, "he told you off his own back."

"Anyway, Abbas," Ali said, as he undid his tie, "Mourat seems to think you could beat me in a game of backgammon."

"I'm not sure about that."

"Would you like a game?" Ali asked.

"I'm not sure," I said as I looked at Mourat for support.

"Go on, Little Man," Mourat encouraged. "It's only a game. You'll thrash him."

"Okay," I said, as a small smile appeared on my face.

Once again, I was sat on the sofa in my favorite spot playing with black, my favorite color, but this time, it against a complete stranger. The only difference this time was that Mourat and the barman were glued to our game. They sat on either side of me and watched like hawks as the game progressed. The game was even more intense than the one I had played with Mourat. No one murmured a word throughout the game. I was pretty lucky with the dice, but I played a good, intelligent game. I beat Ali three games to none. He took it quite well I thought, but from his face, it looked like he was not impressed. As soon as I won the last game, Mourat jumped up and hugged me. I was happy that I had won too, but his reaction seemed a little over the top to me. Ali got to his feet, then threw a bundle of bank notes on the table, and then left without even saying good-bye. Then Mourat picked up the bundle and put it in his pocket. Suddenly, the penny dropped, and I realized what had just taken place. I was so angry that I had been fooled and was so stupid. It all looked strange from the start, and I had been happy just to be playing against someone. I just wanted my time to be occupied. Nevertheless, I felt violated, and it was obvious that I had been taken advantage of. I didn't say anything, so I just looked at Mourat with disgust and walked back into the television lounge.

As I was walking, I heard, "Hey, Little Man, wait up." I ignored it and walked away. I did not want any part of what was going on. I knew that I could not create too much fuss as I was vulnerable, and I was only working out my geography in relation to my hotel. I was adamant that I did not want to move hotels, but I felt really let down by Mourat. Apart from Ahmed, he was the only person that I had trusted a little, and he had let me down. I did not know what to do. So I sat there in the lounge and watched television. After a few minutes, Mourat emerged with a glass of tea.

"Hi, Little Man," he said. I did not respond and pretended I was watching television.

"I brought a glass of tea," he said, trying to put on a more gentle tone.

"I don't want tea, thank you."

"It's on the house," he said with a smile.

I could not believe the man's audacity. I turned to him and quite plainly told him, "I think I have more than paid for all the teas you've given me and more tonight." I spoke to him as a matter of fact and quite abruptly.

He seemed taken back with my perspicacity, but he was man enough to say, "Okay you have a point there." I still continued to ignore him.

"Listen," he said trying to reason with me, "I'm sorry. I really am sorry. It was wrong of me to bet on you without telling you."

"Yes it was," I said. "What would have happened if I had lost?

You would have blamed me."

"No, I wouldn't. I expected you to lose," he said. "He gave me good odds."

Suddenly, I gave him a glare, which he took on board and tried to correct himself. "Well, I didn't expect you to win so comfortably that is all," he explained. "He popped in to see me, and I told him about you beating me, and he said that he would bet that he could thrash me." He paused to see if I was paying any attention to him, which I was.

"So I took the bet. I didn't tell you, because I didn't want you to feel pressured." I still had nothing to say him.

"Listen, would be any better if I gave you ten percent of my winnings?"

Without hesitation, I was in there saying, "Twenty-five."

"What?"

"Twenty-five percent and I'll forgive you."

"You what? You'll forgive me for twenty-five percent?"

"My father says that everything has a price," I said with a smile. I was seeing the funny side to this now, and I was working with an opportunity to make some money.

"Okay," he said with a chuckle, "how about fifteen?"

"How about twenty, and that's my final offer?" He glared at me and then offered his hand so that we could shake.

"You drive a hard bargain, Little Man!"

"I know," I said as I shook his hand. "So how much did you win?"

"Why don't you get straight to the point?" he said sarcastically. "I won thirty thousand lira."

"Crap!" I said. "Okay, you can take one day off my rent and give me one thousand lira in cash. How is that?"

He was laughing out hysterically. "That sounds fine," he said through his laugh. "When did you get time to work all that out in your head?"

I just shrugged my shoulders indicating that I don't know. I then decided that it was time to go and eat my dinner as I had something to celebrate. As I was about to go upstairs, Mourat called me back. "Err, Little Man?"

"Yes?"

"Will you get upset if I ask you something?"

"What?"

"Do you want to do this again?"

"What? Gamble?"

"Yeah," he said in a very soft voice.

"I can't," I explained. "I can't afford to lose money, and my father will not be impressed if he finds out."

"Okay," he said, trying to think and speak at the same time, "what if I gave you an option where you could not lose money?"

"How does that work?"

"Well, I put the money on you, and I find people for you to play, and if you lose, it's my tough luck."

"What? So if I lose, then I would not have to pay anything?"

"Right."

"What?" I asked. "It's that simple, and you would not even be angry with me?"

"No," he said, "I promise, my sole responsibility."

"And if I win?"

"You get a cut, but not twenty percent, because it's all my money to lose."

"How much then?" I asked.

"I was thinking like five percent?"

"Really," I said smiling, "because I was thinking fifteen."

"Ten and that's *my* final offer," he said imitating me.

"Okay, but what about my father?"

"Ah, your father," he said stopping to think. "I mean, does your father really have to know? After all, it's not you who is really gambling, it's me. You'd be just participating in a game, and every so often, I would give you small presents because I like you."

I smiled as I thought about what he was suggesting. He had sold the idea to me. I could save a lot of money if I kept winning and maybe get to eat a little more.

"Deal," I said as I offered my hand.

As we were about to shake on it, I pulled my hand away. "Oh, one more thing."

"What?" he said with a smile, knowing that I had more requests.

"Only one thing, I promise," I said giggling. "Can I have free, unlimited tea?"

"What?"

"You said yourself that you can't play this game unless you drink tea," I explained, "and how am I meant to practice without tea?"

I could see the frustration in his eyes. He was smiling at the same time, but my cheek was really surprising him! He sighed and he said, "Okay, but only if you don't go over the top, and . . ."

" . . . I know, if I don't tell anyone!" as I touched my nose in my customary manner. Mourat chuckled, and he touched his nose too, like it was our little code. I'd like to think that secretly he got a kick from hanging out with me. Mourat turned with a smile and was about to leave me to watch television when I called him back.

"Emm, Mourat?"

"Yes?" he inquired with an about turn.

"Can I have my money please?"

I don't think he could believe his ears. He stood still and looked hard at me, not knowing whether to laugh or cry. "Where have you come from?"

I just laughed. "Well, you do owe me one thousand cash, and one night's free stay."

"That I do."

"Well, my mother always told me not to lend or borrow, and if you don't pay me now, I'll kind of be lending you one thousand," I explained with a smile, "and then I'd have to charge you interest!"

Mourat knew I was joking, but I think he was more shocked at my elementary knowledge of monitory systems. He was obviously not aware of my father's home education!

"Come on, then," he said. "Come and get your money before you kill me!"

I followed him to the reception, where he opened the safe and got a thousand lira note out and handed it to me. In reality, it was not that much money, but it made me happy at the time. I had made my own money, which gave me a lot of self-gratification. I needed all the confidence that I could possibly get. As soon as I took the note off Mourat, I had an idea. I realized that one thousand was not a lot of money, and I did not want it on me, as I would spend it. I wanted to keep it somewhere safe, and this would be a good test to see if Mourat would look after my money without stealing it.

So I turned to him and said, "Can I have an account with you?"

"Sorry?"

"Can I keep the money that I earn in the safe?"

"Sure!" he said with surprise.

"So every time I earn money, we add it to the pile, right?"

"Yeah," he said hesitantly, "so you don't want it now?"

"No, I just wanted to see the money and make sure it is mine!"

"It's okay, Little Man. It's yours!"

"So you'll make a pile just for me in there?"

"Yes, I will."

I knew that I could not carry my dollars on my person for much longer, but I had to make sure that where I kept the money was safe before I changed. I was going to wait to build up a pile of money, and then at a random time, ask for it. If he gave it to me without question, then I would trust him with my dollars too. It was far from a full-proof plan, but it was the best I could come up with at the time.

With a good night's work under my belt, I decided that it was time to reward myself with a meal. I was past hungry, and I was not actually that bothered about food, but I thought should. So I crept up the stairs and made my way to my room. I entered and then went straight for the water. I was quite thirsty. I drank a little and then started to pick the bread. As soon as I started to eat, my appetite returned. I fetched the rest of the yogurt and finished the remainder of my food. It was done all in silence, and the solitude completely broke my mood again. All I could think about was my parents. This was going to be my third night in Istanbul, and they had not called me yet. It was not that late yet, but I was expecting them to call. I tried hard not to cry, and for the first time, I managed to control my feelings. Inside, however, I was not feeling much better. I thought if I returned to the television lounge, time would pass quicker and their call would surprise me.

The rest of the evening, I watched television, but I could not stop turning round every time someone walked in; I still had hope that they would call. The feelings of winning money and my agreements with Mourat seemed like a distant memory. I just longed to hear my mother's voice. I sat there like a lost puppy until I fell asleep.

"Little Man," a voice murmured, "Little Man." It was Mourat trying to wake me up.

"Have I got a call?" I asked, jumping up.

"No," he said with a sad face. "It's late; I thought you might want to go to bed."

"Oh," I groaned despondently, "what time is it?"

"Around four."

"Sorry."

"You don't have to be sorry," he said as a matter of fact. "You can do what you like. I just thought that you'd prefer to sleep in a bed that's all."

"Yeah," I said, "thanks."

I stood up and walked slowly up the stairs. Somehow, I felt let down again. I knew that my father had said he might not call that evening, but I really thought that he would. All I wanted was a little attention. I wished that Mourat had not woken me up, as I was fully awake again. I knew now that I had to go through the arduous routine of getting to sleep again in my room. All I could think about was why my father had not called me. Sure enough, I went through the usual steps of slowly trying to get into the damp bed with the lights on and crying myself to sleep while looking at my family's pictures. It wasn't getting easier.

CHAPTER 9

The next morning I woke up a little later than usual, which made feel better, because I knew that that I had to amuse myself for a little less time. Slowly, I got up and went through the daily routine that I had created for myself. The tedious grooming rituals that had previously been a pain to me seemed like a godsend because it took up time. Very casually and meticulously I washed, brushed, and dressed myself. I knew that I had a trip to the shop to look forward to that day. I had a letter to write, and of course, I had to eat. From the start of the day, these three events were my main motivation to get through it. For the first time, I did not bank on my father calling me. So I decided to concentrate on the things that were certainties.

One could already tell that I was in some sort of routine just by what I was wearing. As I had made myself my base and I was getting a little more comfortable in it, I was not so concerned about dressing as well as I had done previously. I strolled downstairs in my somewhat ripped jeans and took the usual route to Mourat's throne. To my great surprise, it was not him who was sat at reception. It was a much younger man. He was thin, short, and dressed in his best suit, obviously trying to impress. His hair was wet and brushed back. He had classical, dark, Turkish features. The most irritating fact about him was his ever-present pretentious smile. I think that was more a sign of him trying his hardest rather than a part of his personality.

As soon as he saw me, he stood up from his chair and offered his hand. "You Abbas, yes?"

I shook his hand being slightly confused, but I thought that I would go along with it anyway. He kept shaking my hand as he spoke, as if he had forgotten that he was holding it.

"Yes, I'm Abbas."

"Very nice to meet you. I am Hussein."

"Hello," I said as I forced away my hand out of his. His politeness and ever-cheerful manner was making me feel a little uncomfortable.

"Boss said that you will come down, and that I was to give you tea and board."

"You mean Mourat?"

"Yes," he said with an even bigger smile. He then reached under the reception counter and pulled out the backgammon board. "Please take seat, and I bring you tea with sugar." He was pointing to my sofas.

"Okay," I said, not knowing what to do, "but I want to write a letter first to my mother."

"Idiot Hussein," he said as hit himself on the head, "I forgot." He immediately pulled out a ready, stamped airmail envelope and two pieces of paper. He gave it them to me with his already annoying smile. "Just put it here," as he pointed to the reception counter, "when you're done."

"I know."

"Then we can start playing backgammon."

I just looked at him with a fake smile and then retreated to my usual sofa next to the telephones. I couldn't help but to stare at the telephones. I was still hurting on the inside. I could not remember having spent one day without seeing or talking to at least one of my parents.

I realized that I had to concentrate on the positive, at least for the very near future, because I was about to write a letter to my mother. I took my pen and began to write:

Dear Maman,

I hope you and Baba are well. I am really missing you both, especially you because I have not spoken to you for a long time now. But know that I am being good. I have not done anything naughty and am behaving myself! To be honest, I am staying up quite late, but last night it was because I was waiting to see if you or Baba was going to call. You didn't. I think you must have been busy. I am doing well. I have learned how to play backgammon, and I think I am quite good too! I don't have a lot to report today, because I stayed in the hotel all day yesterday. Maybe I will have more to report tomorrow.

I love you,

Your son, Abbas

I slowly sealed the envelope and wrote the address on the envelope. I then approached the reception counter to put the letter in its designated area. As I did so, the ever-cheerful face of Hussein jumped up with the backgammon board.

"How about game now?" I was not really in the mood, but I felt like I had to.

"Okay."

"Good," he said with an overly enthusiastic tone, "I will set it up."

"It's okay," I said as I took the board from him. "I know how."

"Yes," he said, "but you need someone to play with." I suddenly realized what he meant. I did not know that I had to play this guy. This was the last thing that I wanted to do. I did not have any patience for this man. I found him pretentious, overbearing, and quite annoying. I don't remember that game very well. I do not even remember being annoyed by Hussein that much as my mind was somewhere else. I beat Hussein comfortably three games to none. My mind was on the next few days. What was I going to do with myself? How would I cope? I was really missing school, my friends, and living an ordinary life. I was simply not happy. I think I needed more mental stimulation. How little I knew that my daily routine was going to change over the next ten days.

After my game, I went back to the television lounge and reclined in my back-row seat and watched bad, daytime, Turkish television. I eventually drifted off to sleep, and in what had become a custom, Mourat woke me with a gentle tap on the shoulder. I snapped straight out of my snooze to see what he wanted.

"We have work to do, Little Man."

"What?"

"I have a few friends who wish to challenge you," he whispered with his mysterious smile.

"When?"

"When better than the present?"

"Now?"

"Aha," he said with a purposeful nod. "Go and wash your face in the kitchen and meet me in the lounge."

He walked off with a strut. It scared me a little, as he seemed very confident. I was hoping that he had not bet heavily. Even though I was not going to lose anything, I still felt that I was carrying the burden of his gambling. So I did exactly as I was told and walked straight to the kitchen. As I approached, I could hear a lot of noise coming from

127

the lobby. It was like a crowd at a football stadium. I was not sure what was going on, so I decided to ignore it. I went in to find Hussein making about twelve teas.

"Hello, my friend," he said with his ever-annoying smile.

"Hi," I said in a daze. "What is going on?"

"You have spectators today."

"What?"

"Oh, there is big crowd in reception waiting for the little champion."

"Oh, no," I said as I trembled, "this was not in the deal."

"Deal?"

"Nothing," I said quickly. Suddenly, I realized I was scared. I got nervous as it was playing against a stranger, but to play in front of a crowd, too, was going to be challenging. Hussein left the kitchen, and I hovered over the sink not knowing what to do. I was breathing a little heavier and I felt sick. I knew, however, that I had to pull myself together, as there was no way I could back out of this now. I turned the tap on and splashed my face with the chalky, ice-cold water that the Istanbul water authorities had to offer.

Slowly, I staggered outside the kitchen and made my way toward the loud roars. As I made the short walk to the lounge, I peered round the corner first to see what was going to be waiting for me. To my shock, there was a huge man sitting at one side of the board with another ten or twelve people, waving money about like hooligans. In the midst of this crowd was Mourat, orchestrating the event. The man waiting to play must have been 250 pounds, had a receding hairline, a huge moustache, a nose that had been broken at least three times, and very small, sharp eyes. He did not look like the kind of character that one would like to encounter in a dark alley late at night. I was terrified; I knew that I was going to be terrified while playing him, if he was in fact the person that I was going to compete with. I pretty much knew that he was, but I guess I was in denial, trying to make myself believe that it would be someone else. He sat motionless, practicing throwing the little die with his fat, ugly, and chubby hands.

Before entering the arena, I made a conscious decision that if I was to play him, I would not look at him and only stare at the board. With this in mind, I walked into the crowd as if there was no one else there. Once they caught sight of me, a huge roar erupted in the lobby. These men were roaring, shouting, and clapping, as I was an international superstar. I cannot deny that deep inside I liked all the attention, but I was weary that if I did not live up to the hype. I would have been ridiculed.

Mourat walked over to me and whispered into my ear, "They love you, Little Man." I just looked up at him as if I did not care.

"Are you okay?" he asked. I merely nodded my head. The man opposite me was staring at me, but I was sticking to my plan and did not look at him. I did feel intimidated though, because I knew he was staring at me like a wild animal. As soon as Mourat had confirmation from me that I was ready, there was one more eruption of money swapping hands and loud shouting. Then Mourat stopped proceedings by shouting something out loudly in Turkish. Everyone began to stop talking, and the noises simmered down into pure silence. I suddenly knew that it was time for me to take center stage. Again, without looking at the man, I picked up one die and threw it. He got a higher number, and hence, he started the game. I still did not know how much was at stake, but by all the commotion, I gathered that there was a lot of money being circulated. During the first game, I was not relaxed, and I think it must have been obvious. I did not make a fool of myself, but I made certain decisions that I should not have made. I just remember that the crowd was so silent that I almost forgot that they were present. My opponent took the first game from me quite comfortably. I looked up at Mourat, and I could see that he was completely relaxed. To his credit, he smiled at me and nodded to reassure me that all would be okay.

To be fair to Mourat, he played it right with me. His reassurance gave me a little more confidence, which in turn relaxed me. The second game was a tightly fought game, which I just edged. However, as soon as I won, the crowd erupted again. They knew that they had a chance. It was obvious that the odds were against me, which had seduced the punters to bet on me. Because this happened, it suddenly made me think. If these people were betting on me, who was betting against me for Mourat to win our money? I suddenly realized that Mourat was in fact betting against me, and he had given the punters good odds on me. I did not care anymore. I did not care about winning or losing, as he had kept me in the dark again. I looked up at my opponent, and he did not seem so scary anymore. I smiled at him and then gave a glare at Mourat. He must have known that I had caught him in the act again. I think because I did not seem to care, I took the third game with great ease. I really wanted to win, because I wanted to teach Mourat a lesson. Even if I lost, it did not matter because I would win money. To be fair, the third game was won because I had the roll of the die, but I was more at ease.

The fourth game was close again, but my opponent took the game to level it. It was all on the fifth game. The man was sweating heavily. Mourat was looking more edgy and so was the crowd. I did not know what was going to happen, but I really wanted to win. Suddenly, it struck me that I could play dumb and claim money from Mourat anyway. My only mistake had been that I had not asked him how much money he had bet on me previously. Either way, I was to get money out of this. I was in a no-lose situation, and I was beginning to enjoy myself. Once again, Mourat had underestimated me in more ways than one. The fifth and the final game was not close at all. Again, I had good luck with the die, and I played well. It was the quickest game, and when I won, the crowd was going mad. They were screaming, clapping, and one by one they were coming up to me, kissing me, lifting me on their shoulders, and someone even tried giving me beer.

I saw Mourat from the corner of my eye. He was sitting behind the reception counting money out of the safe. He was down, but when his eyes met mine, he tried to hide it. However, I was on to him. I think he knew that I knew, but I was sure that he was not going to say anything until I did. I still did not know how I was going to play it, but I was happy. I had really taught him a lesson. Suddenly, there was a tap on my shoulder. As I turned, I saw my opponent towering over me. He was quite simply massive. I did not want to look at him, but I felt obliged. He offered his hand as if he wanted me to shake it. So like a gentleman, I took his hand, and he smiled as we shook. After this little event, I decided that I would make myself scarce, as I did not want to be near the men when they started to exchange money. It made me feel uncomfortable. So I walked back to the lounge only to be greeted by a load of Persian guests at the hotel. As I entered the lounge, they all cheered. I was really embarrassed as I walked in. I was blushing and went to sit down.

One of the men shouted out, "Hey, kid, what's your name?"

"Abbas."

"Mr. Abbas," he said, "that was some game."

"Thank you," I responded quietly.

"Ah," the man's wife said, "isn't he so cute?"

"Leave the boy alone," her husband retorted. "Where did you learn how to play like that?"

"Here." They all laughed when I said that.

Another man with a more gentle approach asked, "So how long have you been playing?"

"A few days." They all laughed at me again.

"Really?" he asked, "or is that what that guy told you to tell everyone."

"No," I said as a matter of fact. "I promise." I was quite upset that people were not believing me. I could not bear being accused of lying. This had been the fact throughout my short life.

"I'm sorry," the man said apologetically. "Either way, you played a great game. You flew the flag for Persia."

"Thank you."

The lady had been itching to talk for a few seconds, when she could not hold back any longer. "Is it true you are here alone, Sweetness?"

I did not orally respond, as I was not comfortable with everyone knowing my business, but as everyone was looking at me, I nodded to confirm.

"Ahh, you poor baby," she said. "Are you okay?"

"I'm fine," I said, "thank you. I'm sorry I have to go now, but hopefully, I will see you all later. It was a pleasure meeting you all."

Like a rehearsed choir, they all replied, "You too—good-bye."

As I was leaving, I could hear the woman's husband shouting at his wife. "You scared him now," he said. "Couldn't you leave the poor boy alone?"

"What did I do?" she said.

I was out of hearing range as I walked back toward the lounge, but I was smiling at the thought of the couple arguing about me back in the lounge. As I approached the lounge, the last of the crowd was leaving. Mourat caught sight of me early and then came toward me.

"Little Man," he said with his arms open.

"What?"

I thought I could play a sophisticate game with him, but I could not keep my feelings hidden. I was angry with him and there was no hiding it.

"You played a great game, Little Man." He tried to hug me, but I was not in the mood.

"What is it, Little Man?"

"I might not be very old, but I am not stupid, Mourat."

"What do you mean?"

"Okay," I said, "how much money did we win?"

"Well," he said, "that is a good question, around 10,000 Lira."

"Yeah, right!"

"What do you mean?" he asked almost offended.

"I am not stupid, Mourat," I shouted. "I am not doing this any-more."

"What?"

"You heard, you keep trying to cheat me."

"No, I wasn't," he said in a lower tone of voice. "How was I try-ing to cheat you?"

"You thought the fat guy was better than me, but you told your friends that I was quite good. Then you gave them good betting odds on me to win, thinking that I would lose. Then when I lost, you would keep all their money, and I wouldn't know the difference. I would not get any money off my room, and you would walk away with all of it."

"But . . ."

I did not let him talk. "What's more is that you did not bet any of your own money, and I would have felt guilty and would have been upset that I had let you down."

There was a silence as Mourat thought about what I had said.

"Little Man . . ."

"Little Man nothing!" I said. "You lied—again."

I began to walk off when I stopped me physically. "I'm sorry."

"Yeah? Again?"

"I would have given you your cut of the money."

"Sure you would."

"I promise." I just laughed at him.

"You know what?"

"What?" he asked curiously.

"How do you know that the fat guy was not working with one of the guys that bet one me, and he threw the game?"

"Oh . . ."

"Yeah," I said, "you didn't think of that did you when you didn't back me?"

"No."

"Well, you'll never know that will you?"

"I'm so sorry, Little Man; I've learned my lesson now."

"Yeah, whatever."

"Really I am sorry. Please forgive me."

"I forgive you, but I am not playing again."

"What? You have to . . . I need to make money back."

"Not my problem."

"Listen, what can I do to make this up to you?" I just looked at him to see if he was being serious. I was really surprised at his audacity. Then I thought about it, and realized that I could make my own terms here.

"Well, how much money did you lose?"

"One hundred fifty thousand."

"Okay, you have to give my five percent of that for a start."

"What?" he screamed in shock. "But I lost!"

"What's another 7,500 Lira when you've lost 150,000 already?" I asked. Besides, you don't have to pay in cash; you take it off my bill."

"Say I do that," he asked. "Would there be anything else?"

"Yes."

"What?"

"For a start, you always have to bet on me, and there would be no running of books on my games unless you tell me."

"Okay, what else?"

"You always tell me the amount I'm playing for before the game, and I want to see the money."

"Done."

"One more thing."

"What?"

"I want a job."

"You what?"

"I want to work in the hotel on the days that I have nothing to do." I demanded this with my hands on my hips.

"Firstly, I have no money to take anyone on, and if I did, he can't just choose his own days."

"I can."

"But I can't afford to take you on."

"You don't have to," I said. "I've thought about it."

"Oh, yeah, and how does that work? I take it off your bill again?"

"Well that's one option, but I was thinking something different."

"Okay," I said, "I've just seen a lot of your Persian guests, and they all love me."

"If you say so yourself!"

"Well, they do."

"Okay, so what if they do?"

I suddenly brought my voice down and whispered, "Well, they feel kind of sorry for me, at least their wives always do."

"Get to the point.'"

"Okay," I said, "hold on. You see, I can be the tea boy. If I am the one selling the teas, they will order more and just put it on their tabs, and then they will pay me tips. You make more money with better tea sales, and I will make extra money with my tips."

Mourat just looked at me as if he was at a loss for words.

"Are you really seven?"

"Almost eight."

"Okay, it sounds good, but I'm only agreeing on a temporary basis to see if it works."

"Fine."

"But if I want you to play backgammon, that will take priority."

"And I choose my own hours."

"Done."

"So you're taking 7,500 off my bill?"

"Yeeeeeees."

"I have it all written down, you know?"

"Oh," he said with a chuckle, "I would expect nothing less."

I decided that I needed to go and get food before it got dark. I left the hotel lounge and headed for the corner shop. I was in a good mood as I had everything that I wanted out of the situation. It was obvious that Mourat needed me more than I needed him. This made negotiating with him a lot easier. I was pretty proud of myself.

I entered the shop, and this time the smell of the kavourma was too tempting. I decided that I deserved some meat after two days of bread and yogurt. I bought the loaf of bread, two bottles of water, a pot of yogurt, and a kavourma sandwich. Ufundy recognized me immediately,

"Kavourma today, Little Man?"

"Yes," I responded, "it is Friday." He chuckled to himself as he took great care over his toasted masterpiece.

He handed it to me, and in his broken Farsi said, "Enjoy, Little Man."

"Thank you, Ufundy," I said. "Good-bye."

"Good-bye."

When I returned to the hotel, the sun was about to go down. I did not really want to eat yet, as it was too early, but I did not want my kavourma to get cold, and so I retired in my room and enjoyed every crumb of my toasted sandwich. It really was tasty, especially after bread and yogurt. I was still not getting used to eating alone. I always looked forward to eating as I was on one meal a day. I was always hungry, and I tried to eat as slowly as possible to make the experience last longer. However, it was also one of the saddest parts of my day. It was only better than going to sleep. I really missed my family at meal times. It was a time where my loneliness was highlighted. When I was busy, I didn't think about my parents, but at that particular time, they were all I thought about. I wondered if they would call that night. My father had promised me that he would, but I was not sure anymore. I was very angry and disappointed with my father at that time. I felt he had let me down. I guess it was part of my selfish immaturity. I didn't consider how he was feeling, because I was scared. I really missed my mother too. I still felt as close to her though as I had always been. I just did not know what to expect next. If they were to call that evening, I wondered if I would be able to speak to my mother, and I thought about telling them about my new job. Then and there, I decided not to, in case it did not work out. I did not want to disappoint my father. Thinking back on it, it was a funny position. I felt let down by him, and yet I yearned so much for his respect.

After my dinner, I staggered down the pungent stairs and took my position in the lounge. It was beginning to fill up as everyone was coming back after his or her day's business. I decided that it was good time to start working. I went to reception to find Mourat, feeling sorry for himself.

"Mourat?"

"No more conditions—you're killing me."

"No, I just wanted to know where I write down people's drink tabs."

"Oh," he said in a surprised tone, "you're starting now?"

"When better than the present?"

"Yeah, very funny, Little Man," he said in his sarcastic manner. "You know what your trouble is?"

"No what?"

"You don't act your age."

"I'm only seven, though."

"I know. That's my point. You should try acting seven rather than thirty-seven."

I just laughed at him.

"No, I'm serious," he said. "This is just scary."

"Okay," I said still chuckling, "but where do I write down the tabs?"

"The tab list is behind the bar," he said with a sigh. "I'll show you." He led me through to the bar, which was located at the right hand side of the television lounge. He took me behind the bar.

"Okay," he said, "you see this list?"

"Yeah."

"You just write down what they have next to their room number."

"So it's not just tea?"

"It's evening now, so not everyone will want tea," he said as a matter of fact, "but try and keep it down to tea if you can."

"Okay," I said, a little unsure.

"It's okay. If you're unsure about anything, just come and ask me."

"Okay."

Suddenly, I realized that everyone in the lounge was looking at us. Mourat saw this and like the fox that he was, he decided that he should announce my new position.

"Ladies and gentleman," he declared, "may I introduce our new barman and tea boy."

He pointed at me, and the crowd all began to clap. Why they did that, I am not sure, but I think they were trying to make me feel good. I gave Mourat my glare that made him realize that he was in trouble, and so he tried to fix it by saying, "And may I also say that he only earns the tips that you may wish to give him."

I hit Mourat on the leg when he said that, as it made me look desperate, but I was happy that he did it, because I did not want to say it myself.

"Good luck, Little Man." And that was that. Mourat went back to his throne, and I was left behind the bar. There was a little pause before the lady from earlier waved me over to her. I walked over to her and she touched my head.

"You are so cute," she said. "I want to take you home with me."

I just smiled at her and hoped that she wanted to order some drinks. Unfortunately, she did not, so I just asked her, "Can I get you a drink, madam?"

"Ah, he's so polite too," she told her husband.

"Can't you just leave the boy alone. He's not a toy."

"I want to order a drink." She had pleased me at last. She was really kind lady, but I just wanted to make money. It seemed as if I had to play up to her more and more.

"I want a tea and so does he," as she pointed to her husband.

"No, I don't," he snapped. "I want a beer."

"Okay."

I went to the kitchen and poured the tea and got some sugar cubes and a teaspoon, which I placed on the saucer next to the small glass of tea. Then I went to the bar and opened the fridge to see if I could find beer. I saw a few different types and chose what I had seen people drink the most. There was a bottle opener on the counter. I opened the bottle and put a glass next to it on the tray and took the drinks over to the couple. I put it next to them but did not wait to be tipped, as I was too embarrassed. I waited to be called back by the lady, but it was in fact the man that spoke. "Hey, kid?"

"Yes, sir?"

"Come here a second."

I walked back to him, and he gave me 100 Lira. It was not a huge amount of money, but it was a fair enough tip. I did not even expect that much. If I served only ten drinks and got a similar tip, I worked out that it would pay twenty percent of one night's stay. Then I returned to the bar to write down the drinks on the couple's tab. I had forgotten to ask for their hotel room. So I returned to them to ask, but I approached the lady as I was more intimidated by the man.

"Excuse me, madam?"

"Yes, Sweetness?"

"What is your room number so that I can put the drinks on your tab?"

"Thirty-seven."

"Thank you, madam."

I saw her gesture to another couple, implying that I was cute again. As she did this, another man shouted over to me,

"A beer for me too. Please, kiddo," he said, "and don't worry about the glass. Room 12."

I liked people like him. He was trying to make my life as easy as possible. So I returned to the bar and wrote down his order on the tab and returned with his bottle to find that he had 150 Lira waiting for me. Then the orders began to come in thick and fast, until I was rushed off my feet. However, something else that was happening was that the crowd in the lounge was competing with each other in typical Persian fashion. Instead of keeping the tip at 100 Lira, they were all trying to outdo each other with slightly higher tips until I reached my maximum tip of the night of 350 Lira. This seemed ridiculous, but I was making money. I also knew for a fact that Mourat would be happy as he was selling a lot of drinks, and he made good money on his drinks. Most people were drinking beer, which made it easy for me. A few of the ladies drank tea, which was easy too.

I was amongst the guests as they were talking to me and placing more orders when Mourat came into the lounge.

"Abbas," he shouted, "you've got a phone call."

"Oh," I said, "can you take over for me until I get back?"

"Sure."

I put my tray down and ran toward the phone in the lobby. I had been so busy I had completely forgotten about my parents. I ran into the booth and closed the door behind me.

"Maman?"

"Abbas," my father's deep resonating voice echoed down the line, "it's me."

"Is Maman there? Can I speak to her today?"

"No, Son," he said, "not today."

"Why not?" I demanded an answer and was being quite insolent.

"Because I said so." That was the end of that conversation. There was a silence as I waited to hear what he had to say. "I'm sorry I did not call yesterday, Abs, but . . ."

"It's okay."

"Yeah—listen, your mother is really worried about you, and I don't want her to be worried more."

"I'm fine; I'll tell her that, Baba. I promise."

"I know, I just don't think that . . ."

" . . . Have I ever told you that it's horrible here? Have I not done everything that you told me to do?"

"Yes, but it's not that simple, Abs."

"I know—I'll find out when I'm older right?"

"Something like that."

There was another pause. I did not know what to say to him, as he was not really saying the things that I wanted to hear.

"So how are you, Abs?"

"I'm okay." I said trying to hold back my tears. I really wanted to tell him that I am lonely and miss them all, but there was no point as I felt that he would be even more disappointed in me. I thought that he was disappointed in me because he was not really saying anything encouraging to me. "Things are going well. I wrote a few letters to Maman, and I watch a lot of television and don't leave the hotel unless I have to—just like you told me to."

"Good lad."

"So, do you know when I am getting my papers?"

"Well, I sent them all together today by express, and they should be with you within five to ten days—that is what the man at the post office told me."

"Okay," I said despondently, "so when will I be able to speak to Maman?"

"Soon."

"Okay, but will you send her my love?"

"Of course, I will."

"Okay, Baba. Go before your bill gets huge."

"Yeah," he said with a huge pause before his next words, "you take care, Son."

"I will."

"I'll try and call you soon."

"Sure—call when you can. Don't worry about me. I'll be fine."

"Bye, Son."

"Bye, Bab . . ." and with that, he hung up the phone. Once again, tears were rolling down my cheeks. I sat on the stool and dried my eyes before leaving again. I peeped my head round the corner to see that no one could see me. I then ran into the kitchen and washed my face so that no one could tell I had been crying.

Suddenly, Mourat came in with a tray of empty glasses. "Where have you been?"

"On the phone."

"What did you do to these people, they are ordering and drinking beer like animals." I smiled at this. I needed a bit of good news.

"You've got the job for as long as you want it."

"Thanks."

"This is great business, Little Man. You're cleverer than you look."

"I know."

"Modest too." I chuckled.

"You better get back out there before they start demonstrating."

"Okay." I was about to leave when Mourat called me back.

"Little Man?"

"Yeah?"

"Some of the guests were keen that you got this," he said as he handed me a bundle of small notes. It was my tips that I had not collected. My bundle was quite big now. I certainly needed that kind of boost, because the conversation with my father had really depressed me. I was about to leave again when Mourat called me once more.

"Little Man?"

"Yeah?"

"Good job."

"Thanks," I said pensively as I looked at him walk away.

I was slightly happier that night as I had made some money, I didn't feel all that bored, and I was genuinely ready for bed. I was very tired from the work. The excitement and the adrenaline had kept me going, but I did not get to my room until well past three o'clock in the morning. I had a smile on my face right until I opened my room. I was determined that his would be my first night not to cry to sleep. Even with all the excitement of the job and my popularity throughout the hotel, there was nothing that could replace my parents. It was love and real attention that I was missing. It was at these times that I missed my mother. Still bedtime was the loneliest part of the day for me. I went through my nightly rituals, and once again, I ended up in bed with the pictures of my family. I was tired, but every time I ended up in this position, my heart always increased in pace and felt like it had missed a beat. As this happened instantaneously, my eyes would swell up, and without my knowledge make their way onto the already damp sheets. Luckily, on that particular night, I was tired and before I knew it, I was fast asleep.

CHAPTER 10

I woke up quite early considering how late I had gone to sleep. From the moment I opened up my eyes, I knew that this was a strange day. I did not know why because the sun was shining, the noises from the street were far below their scary levels, and for the first time, I had a smile on my face at the beginning of the day. Previously, I had been just as scared from boredom as anything else. Now I knew that I had things to do to stimulate my mind. I felt like I was useful and had a purpose, slight as it was. I did not make huge amounts of money, but it was way above anyone's expectations, and that alone gave me motivation to continue. I had a letter to write, and I had backgammon to play and tea to serve when my mood was agreeable. Throughout my short life, it had been money that I had chased, and therefore, any small enterprise that saw cash at the end of the tunnel motivated me.

As I was getting changed, I noticed the usual cockroaches running around the edges of my miniscule room and of course in the bathroom. I noticed that I was no longer as scared of them as I used to be. Admittedly, I was not exactly fond of them, but they did not horrify me anymore. I had got used to living in the same habitat as them. I don't think that it was because I was suddenly any tougher physically, but I had adapted a little because I had no other choice. Mentally, I was more alert, and I had to be because I knew that there were people there who would not hesitate to take advantage of me. Even my closest ally, or so I thought, had tried to do that very thing before my own eyes. Though I was more secure in my surroundings, I knew that was still very vulnerable and that I still maintained a degree of paranoia within me. Even at my best, I felt weak and scared. Mentally, that is a very hard thing to deal with as you are always looking out. I cannot say that I didn't sleep, but my sleep pattern was nothing like what it had been in the security of my real home in Tehran. I found that one needs a lot of mental strength to deal with paranoia, and the only way that I dealt with it was by keeping myself busy.

Before taking the trip down the stairs, I decided to take my money out of my pockets and check my financial situation. I also had a small notepad with what I was owed to me by Mourat and the money that I had with him. I was pretty happy with the situation, as most of my money was still intact, but I did not have all that much in Lira. I therefore decided that I would take another trip to the town center and see what rate I could get. I was quite looking forward to seeing Hector. He had been so good to me before, but I had learned from Mourat that I still could not trust those who were nice to me. I made my mind up to go and see what rates everyone else would give me prior to my visit to Hector's shop. Then I would know whether he was giving me a good rate or not.

I walked down the stairs, and to me relief, it was Mourat on duty. He was half-asleep in his usual manner behind the reception counter. I did not even ask for the stationary as he handed it to me upon my arrival. I went over to my spot and began to write to my mother again. It was perhaps the most melancholy of my letters, but I was frustrated that I was not speaking to my mother. I felt like I really needed her.

Dear Maman,

I hope you are well. I am doing okay. Days are passing by slowly. I am still waiting for the papers that Baba is sending to me. However, I cannot help but to feel a little sad as I have not spoken to you for a very long time. Every time I ask Baba, he tells me that I can speak to you next time, and it does not happen. I know that I am meant to be a man now, but I do miss you, Maman. I really miss you. I have not got a lot more to report apart from the fact that I am doing fine. Do not worry about me; I'm okay. I just would like to speak to you, that is all.

I love you,

Your son, Abbas

It was a short letter, but I think I had got my point across. I really wanted to tell my mother about my jobs and how well I was doing, but I knew that it could backfire if my father found out. Actually, I wanted to tell him too—but I was too scared. If he had found out, maybe he would have been more proud of me. At that particular time, I was feeling very neglected by my father. By this, I meant that I felt like I needed more emotional support. Having said that, should he have been softer, I would not have faired as well.

When I placed my sealed and addressed envelope in its appropriate position, Mourat reached over with the backgammon board. However, I put my hand out to decline. Up until that point, Mourat had been too tired to try to converse with me, but now, like a breath of fresh air, he opened his mouth.

"A champion needs to practice."

"Yes, but a champion also needs to have Lira!"

"Ah," he said, "I can swap money for you."

"It's okay," I said. "I have a contact in town who gives me the best rate!"

"Oh really?"

"Yeah."

"And who is that?"

"Just a friend," I said with a smile. "His name is Hector."

"Hector, huh," he questioned with that suspicious smile of his, "and what rate did he give you last time?"

"One thousand."

Mourat did not respond for a few seconds, and then after careful internal deliberation he decided to ask, "What about the tea?"

"What about it?"

"Well, someone has to serve it."

"I don't think my customers will be up anytime soon, as they went to bed late."

"Your customers now, eh?" he asked sarcastically.

"You know what I mean."

"Yeah," he said laughing, "I'm just fooling around. But seriously, what if someone does want tea?"

"Then someone else has to serve it to them, as I will be out until lunch time," I said as a matter of fact. "Besides, the agreement was that I choose my own hours."

Mourat knew that I had him on the last point.

"Yeah, I guess we did make that arrangement," he said in defeat, only to raise his voice again with excitement as he thought of something new, "but we did say you are working on a trial basis."

"Until you said that I have the job time as long as I want it last night."

"I said that?" he asked with a knowing tone. "The problem with you is . . ."

145

" . . . that I don't act my age. I know!"

"Yeah, that too," he said with a chuckle, "but I was going to say that your memory is too good."

"That means I have two big problems now!"

"I guess it does," he said smiling. "Now off with you. The sooner you go, the sooner you will return."

"I want to come back soon," I explained. "I want to make money."

"Oh, believe me," he said sarcastically again, "I kind of got that gist awhile back."

"Okay, I'm off now."

"Do you know where you're going?"

"Yeah, I think so," I said. I had suddenly lost my confidence a little. "I turn left here until I hit the main road, and then turn right until I reach the indoor market. Is that right?"

Mourat looked at me and said nothing. He did smile at me, but he didn't say anything. He was so strange sometimes.

"Well, is it right?" I asked.

"Spot on." With that, I waved good-bye to him and left the hotel.

As relieved as I was to leave the hotel, my mood immediately changed once I stepped outside the doors of the hotel. I needed to get out for my own sanity, but I really didn't feel comfortable alone on those streets. The further I walked away from the hotel, the busier the street became. Once again, I had to make my way through the hoards while keeping my hands in my pockets to protect my money. I was being barged from right to left and vise versa. It felt a little rougher than my previous visit, but it was nothing that phased me. I was expecting it, which made the experience a little more bearable. The main street that led to the market was so busy that I could not see further than five feet ahead of me. I really did not want to be there, but I did have to swap money. My intentions were clear from the outset: go inside the market, go past Hector's shop without being detected, and then get three or four rates from different shops. Then I was to return to Hector's and decide on what to do. On getting my Lira, I was going to go straight back to the hotel. As always, things did not pan out the way I had envisioned them.

I managed to get through the crowds and arrived at the market gates in very little time. I thought the time of my journey seemed to be less than last time because I was thinking too much. I went through different scenarios in my head, and at the same time, suspected everyone of wanting to mug me. Within the boundaries of the hotel, my paranoia was bad enough, but on the outside, it reached very high levels. I stopped at the gates and decided to think about how I was going to pass Hector's shop. The likeliness of me being seen by him was very low, but I wanted to make sure. A group of American tourists were gathering very near me, and their guide began to lead them inside. This was perfect for two reasons. Firstly, I could hide among them, and secondly, no one would bother me, as they would think that I was with my parents. This would, therefore, make them think that it was my parents that had the money and not me. Well, at least one of my theories seemed to work. Hector definitely did not get a sight of me, but the market traders certainly had no problems about bothering me with their furniture. I would have thought that the laws of common sense would have taught the traders that seven-year-old boys do not tend to be interested in carved furniture. Perhaps it was me that did not have the common sense.

I went from jeweler to jeweler, and once again, no one would unsettle the status quo. I was getting a standard rate of 980 Lira everywhere. Even though my geography of the market was much better and I was moving with more ease, internally I was still far from comfortable. I wanted to do my business as quickly as possible and get out of the vicinity. This, therefore, only meant one thing. I walked hesitantly toward Hector's shop door. I was about to open it when he caught sight of me. With great enthusiasm and energy, he bounced to the door and opened it for me.

"Abbas, my friend," he said, "welcome back."

"Thank you."

"Please, please, come in my friend," he said with the respect and curiosity that one pays a king. "Pepsi or Fanta?"

"Sorry?"

"What would you like to drink? Pepsi or . . ."

"Really, Hector," I said, interrupting him mid-flow, "I've just come for . . ."

"Today's rate, right?" he interrupted back. He was so enthusiastic. It was almost abnormal. It was, however, a pleasant change for me. It felt good to be recognized and treated like a human being.

"That's right."

"I'll give you 1100 Lira per dollar, and I'll guarantee . . ."

"I'll take it," breaking into his sentence once again.

"That was easy—what is it? Are you no longer cautious?"

"No," I said with a smile, "I have already checked what everyone else is offering."

"You're a clever one," he said with a smile. "I told you that before; you're certainly clever."

"I'll take $50 worth please."

"Sure," he said all seriously, "but please, have a drink with me first." I looked at my Casio watch and saw that I had plenty of time. I could even have two drinks, and I would still be back in time for the lunch rush back at the hotel. I was just concerned that I would not lose out on my tips at lunchtime.

"Okay," I said. "I'll have a Fanta, please."

"Fanta coming up."

Hector was about to walk, when I said, "Sorry, Hector?"

"Yes," he said with a smile on the turn.

"How much will that be?"

"What? The Fanta?" he asked in astonishment.

"Yes," I said in a lowered and embarrassed whimper.

"My friend," he proclaimed, "you are my guest. When I offer you a drink, I ask you as a guest. It is free, of course."

"Oh," I sighed blushing, "I see. I'm sorry, Hector. You just don't know who to trust."

Suddenly, a look of sadness appeared in his deep brown eyes. I almost saw tears well up in them. He stood motionless for seemed like an eternity looking hard at me with that melancholic expression. I did not know what to do or say. Therefore, I stayed silent and lowered my head in shame, not knowing which of my words that had brought about such an atmosphere into the air. Then I decided to speak, as I could not bear that sad stare anymore.

"I'm sorry if I said anything, sir, that . . ."

"It's not you, my child." There was a pause as he chose his words carefully. This was the first time someone had referred to me as a child since my Turkish adventure had begun. I had liked Little Man more, but the way that he carried such affection in his words—I seemed not to care. "It's just so tragic that the truth about our world today breeds such early cynicism in today's youth."

"Oh," I said, pretending I understood what he was talking about.

"Wait one second while I get the Fanta."

I sat on a little stool in the shop and tried to think about what he had said. I could not really understand it, but I got the rough meaning just from the way he said it. In retrospect, I do not think that I would have been as skeptical had I not been in a position where I had no other choice. Suddenly, I looked up at the doorway to find Hector looking at me still with his sad eyes. I stood up and walked over to him. I reached out and took the bottle of Fanta away from him.

"Thank you," I said plainly and returned to my stool.

"My pleasure."

"So," I said, casually trying to make conversation, "have you been busy today?"

"Fair to good, I guess."

"Good," I said as I took a sip. Something that sticks in my mind at around this point was the fact I saw a hole in the crotch area of my jeans. I remember trying to try hide the hole rather than listening to what Hector was saying or doing. Once again, I was in a hurry to leave the shop. I drank my Fanta in big gulps and was waiting for the appropriate time to make my excuses. Hector said something that completely changed the events of that day.

His words were very precise. "Abbas," he said pensively, "I was going to ask you if you wanted a small job once or twice a week, but I don't want to do that any more."

I really cannot make my mind up if he meant it or not, as he was such a lovely man. Yet the cynical side of me fails to believe that this was not a baiting line. Whether it was or not, I fell for it hook, line, and sinker.

"What job?" I asked like an idiot. Admittedly, age was not on my side, but I should have known better. I was more intelligent than this, but I guess one is never wise. One can only get wiser.

"No, really," he protested, "it really doesn't matter." Of course, the more he protested, the more my curiosity got the better of me.

"No, tell me. What was it?"

"It was nothing," he said. "It was a simple job."

"What?" I demanded.

"All it was," he explained with a throwaway manner, "was that you would have to take a parcel half a mile to another shop down that same road that you got the bus from."

"What's in the parcel?" I asked.

"That I cannot tell you," he said sharply. "You would not be allowed to open the parcel either."

"How much?"

"$20."

"All I have to do is walk half a mile with this parcel, and you would give me $20 US?"

"Aha."

"What's the catch?"

"There isn't one," he said. "It's just a confidential delivery; that's all."

I could not believe my ears. This was too good to turn down.

"So how big is this parcel? Is it heavy?"

"God no," he said with a smile. "Look." He got a parcel all ready out from behind the left counter. It was square-shaped, about 30 centimeters by 30 centimeters and around 10 centimeters high.

"I'll do it."

"What, now?"

"When better than the present?" I was sure that Mourat would not mind me using his phrase.

"Are you sure?"

"Yes," I said excitedly, "but I get paid now right?"

"No," he explained. "I give you $10 now, and the man you will deliver it to will give you another $10 when he receives the parcel."

"Okay."

"So you know where you got the bus from, right?"

"Yes," I said as if this were drinking water for me.

"Good," he went on, "you take that road, and walk around 500 meters up that little hill and along the row of shops on the right-hand side of the road. You'll eventually come to a launderette."

"Okay."

"There you will see a very large man. His name is Abdul," he said. "You are only to give the money to him. If he is not there, then bring the parcel back, and I will still give you the rest of your money."

"That is fair," I said. This really was too good to be true.

"One more thing."

"What?" I asked.

"If you think anyone is watching you or following you, do not under any circumstances go to the launderette. Do you understand?"

"Yes," I said a little frightened, "but why would anyone follow me?"

"I'm just saying."

"Oh," I said pretending to understand, but it did not make any sense. I did not mention it again, though, because $20 was a lot of money to me. "So if anyone does follow me, do I bring the parcel back here?"

"No," he said almost having a heart attack. He then returned to the counter and got a little card out. "You take this card," he ordered, "and if that does happen, go to your hotel and ring me on this number. Okay?"

"That is easy enough."

"Good."

"So do I have to report back here if it is delivered?"

"No," he said calmly, "you can go home."

"But how do I prove that I delivered the parcel?"

"That is a good question, Abbas," he said with a smile. "Your proof is the $10 bill that he will give to you."

"But that could be any $10 bill," I said. I was not that stupid. "What if I want to spend it?"

"The bill has some writing on it with pencil in one of the corners." He explained, "You can spend my bill, and then next week, if we do this again, I'll give you another bill for the penciled one, plus the $10 for next week's delivery." I stood still and thought about what he was suggesting.

"So really I only get half of my money this week?"

"No, you get all of it this week," he said, "but if you want your proof, you can't spend half for one week that is all."

"Okay," I said as I thought about what he had said. "So can I have my $10?"

"Sure," he replied. With that, he pulled out the biggest bundle of dollars I had ever seen. He had ever denomination possible. He must have had at least five or ten thousand dollars in his pocket. I was certainly impressed.

I took my money and the parcel and made my way through the crowds onto the street to the bus stop that I had used to get to the consulate. Now I was even more worried. I was still worried about my own money, but now I had the extra responsibility of the parcel too. I did not know what was inside, and I obeyed my instructions about not opening it. I knew, however, that it must have been valuable. Otherwise, they would not be paying me so much. I knew deep down that what I was doing was wrong, but the temptation of the money was too much, and I did not know how long I was going to be residing in Istanbul. What I knew for sure was that out of all my jobs this would be the one that my father should never find out about. I tried to justify my actions to myself as one does when doing something wrong. The way I did this was that I was doing what I had to do to survive. I did have money, but I didn't know how long it was going to last. My other two jobs were good, but they did not pay anywhere as much as this one. It was very easy money, but my mother's old proverbs used to ring inside my head. She used to say that easy money was the devil's money!

As I walked up the small hill, I kept turning round to see if anyone was in fact following me. I was sweating heavily because I was very scared. My heart was racing, and I was walking very fast. This certainly did not help my paranoia in any shape or form. I was just thinking about the $20, and all of a sudden, it did not seem such a good idea. It was far too late now, and I did not dare go back to Hector's shop. I was probably closer to the launderette now.

Before long, I suddenly noticed a dingy, little launderette. It was small and it was really dark inside. I looked behind me and to the sides for the final time. I then crossed the road to the opposite side. I walked twenty yards and then crossed back to the side of the launderette and returned to it. I did not know what I had achieved, but it seemed like the right thing to do at the time. I looked through the window, and it was so dark that I could not see the far side of the shop. I did not really want to go inside, but I knew that I had to. I opened the door slightly, and immediately, I jumped up as a bell sounded with the opening of the door. I tried to calm myself before walking any further. I could not really imagine anyone using that launderette to clean clothes. It stank of cigarette smoke, and there was mold all over the walls. The floor was sticky, and as I walked across it, it squelched. My heart was racing even faster now, and my rate of perspiration could not possibly have been normal.

As I walked through the thick, pungent smoke, I saw who must have been Abdul. He must have been over three hundred pounds. He was reclined in a fat leather chair that had its stuffing popping out of various holes. He had a completely bent nose, which undoubtedly had been broken very badly. His moustache was old school and curled at the ends. He had heavy stubble, and his sideburns needed a trim. He was sweating far heavier than me, but it did not seem to bother him. There was a little fan in front of him keeping his head cool. He had a used handkerchief in the top pocket of his cotton shirt. I could see his rolls of flab popping through his tight yellow shirt. I was terrified as he stared at me. I did not want to say anything, but he was looking at me in complete silence. So I decided to take the initiative.

"Excuse me, sir?" I inquired in my faintest and politest of voices. "Are you Abdul?"

"Aha," he grunted in a deep and truly terrifying voice.

"I have this for you." I gave him the parcel. He took it very gently from my hands, and then with great effort he got up from his seat. He looked at me with a glare as drops of sweat made their way down his face, and then he looked at the parcel.

"Don't go anywhere."

He then very slowly disappeared through his back door. He did not go far from the door as every one of his footsteps made a clear, distinctive sound. He then reappeared from behind the door, but without a parcel. He leaned forward over the counter. My heart literally stopped as I thought he was going to hurt me. Instead, he opened his hand and offered me what was, in fact, a $10 bill. Very slowly, I took it from him, and then like a fool, I decided to inspect it. I opened the note up, and sure enough, there was five-digit number written in one of the corners in pencil. Abdul was looking at me hard, but I seemed to be paralyzed. My feet were not moving. I had no further business there, but I did not know for sure that I was free to go.

"What else do you want? A kiss?" His voice was so resonant and deep. I had to think hard about what he was saying, when I realized that I could go.

"Oh, sorry," I stuttered. "I mean, thank you. Thank you, sir."

I backpedaled toward the door through the smoke and tried not to let Abdul out of my sight. When I reached the door, I very gently opened the door and very calmly walked down the hill toward the bus stop. As soon as I was out of Abdul's sight, I began to run. I had never been so scared before in my life. Now I was happy. I had my $20, and after all that effort, it was worth it. After all, it had only been forty-five minutes of work. That was more than my father was getting at that particular time. Yet the morality of how I got the money never did leave the back of my mind.

I made my way back to the hotel as quickly as I could, as I was already late for the lunchtime rush. I only wanted to get back for my own sake, as it was me that was missing out on the tips. However, anything that I had missed had more than been made up with my $20. It was never enough for me, though. I wanted to make as much money as possible. For the first time, I had to get somewhere in a hurry. I felt important, and I loved that feeling of having completed one job and rushing to another. For the entire length of my journey home, I was gloating in my success, but at the same time, I could not help but to be curious as to what was in that parcel. I was walking briskly, and I had my hands in my pockets to protect my money, as usual. My head was down, and I was going through the crowd trying to mind my own business. Suddenly, a huge thud smacked across my shoulders. I was knocked back and onto the floor. A small space appeared amongst the crowd. A man had been walking fast in my direction, and because my head was down, I had not gotten out of his way. His shoulder caught mine, and I ended up the worse for it. However, the man was furious. He walked up to me and started to shout at me in Turkish. I was so scared, as he was towered over me. I was still on the floor.

I tried to apologize. "I'm sorry, sir," I said.

As soon as he heard me speaking Farsi, he became even more angry. He then leaned over me and picked me up by one of my ears. He said something about Iranians, but I could not understand anymore. I guess it was not very pleasant. Then out of nowhere, he slapped me right across my face. I remember wanting cry my eyes out, but I really felt a feeling of hate for that man. It was feeling of hate that I had never had for anyone before. I had disliked people before, but I never hated before. If anyone had given me a knife, I would have killed him without hesitation in the heat of the moment. He had insulted me. He had hit me for a petty reason, which I had tried to apologize for, and he had said something about my race. This was my first experience of racism, and ironically enough, it was from a Turk. The man then spat on my head and walked away. Everyone had stopped to watch what he was doing, and yet no one had bothered to help me. I felt so humiliated, and the pain of feeling like the outsider was worse than the pain of his slap, which incidentally was very hard. As soon as I was away from the incident, I checked my pockets for my money. I was so relieved that it was there. Then my mind was taken away from this as the man's saliva began to drip down my forehead. The disgust and hate that I was feeling was beyond any words. There had been nothing that I could have done to stick up for myself as the man simply overpowered me physically. I slowly put the end of my sleeves over my hands and wiped his spit from my head. I rubbed and rubbed, but I knew that I had to have a shower before I could do anything.

As I turned off the main road onto the road of the hotel, I could not hold back my tears. I could not remember why I was so upset. I was certainly in shock as the whole event had taken me by complete surprise. My face was stinging, but I really did not care about that. There was something that hurt inside me, but I could not understand what it was. It was more than the humiliation that I felt. Perhaps it was the fact that I was the outsider and alone. I had never experienced this before, and I could not talk to my parents about it either. Trying to work out these things by myself was confusing and hurtful. I really needed some type of mentor or guidance at this point. I knew that I could not confide in my parents, as their guilt would be multiplied.

It was after one when I stepped back into the hotel. I had wiped away my tears, and I was trying to focus on the next task at hand. Mourat was there in his seat, waiting like a parent whose child had missed curfew.

"What time do you call this?"

"I told you before," I snapped firmly, "the agreement was that

I choose my own hours. Besides, I told you that I would be back by lunchtime, and it's lunchtime."

"Okay," he said, taken back by my abruptness. "I was only joking."

"Sorry," I said softly, "I'll need ten minutes before I can start work." Mourat suddenly got up in a strange manner as he looked at me. He spoke, but I could see that he was concentrating on what he was observing, rather than what he was saying,

"Sure, take your time," he said staggering toward me. It was making me feel kind of uncomfortable, but I decided not to say anything. Mourat slowly closed the distance between us in the lobby, and then reached his hand forward toward my face very slowly. I wanted to flinch, but I stood my ground. Mourat tilted my head to one side. I tried resisting, but it was pointless.

"What happened to your face?"

"What do you mean?" I asked innocently.

"It's completely red on one side," he said. "What happened?"

"Nothing," I responded softly with my head down.

"Did someone hit you?"

"No."

"Then what happened?" he demanded. "Was it when you were swapping money?"

"No, I got my money," I said. "I got 1100 Lira per dollar." There was no gloating in my last statement. It was spoken softly, and I was desperately trying to think of something to avoid further interrogation. I could not possibly allow Mourat to know that I had been hit, and that I was vulnerable. The image that I had always portrayed in front of him had been one of overconfidence and as a bright intelligent boy who knew exactly what he was doing.

"Okay," he said, "but I know that something did happen."

"Listen, Mourat," I said, "I need to go upstairs for ten minutes, and then I will come down, and I'll do my job. Is that okay?"

"Take as long as you need."

"Thank you."

I walked quickly out of the lobby and onto the stairs where I slowed down again. I really did not feel like doing anything. All I wanted to do was get into the shower. I made my way into the room and immediately took all my clothes off. I then entered the shower and began washing my hair with shampoo. I repeated this procedure at least five times. I wanted all traces of that man to leave me. I kept going over to the mirror to check that there was no more saliva on me. Eventually, I assumed a position in the shower, and I did not want to leave it. I even sat on the floor under the warm water. I do not know what it was about the water that made me feel a little better, but I felt a little safer there. As I was getting used to being alone, something happened that had opened my eyes again. I realized once again that there was no one to protect me and look after me anymore.

Eventually, I got back into the room and began to put fresh clothes on. A knock at my door made me jump. I did not know what to do, and so I ignored the knock. After a few seconds, there was another knock.

I ignored it again, only to hear Mourat. "Little Man?" he called, "Little Man, are you there?"

"Yeah," I responded softly, "hold on." I continued to finish dressing quickly and then partially opened the door. Mourat was there with a bag of ice.

"Can I come in, Little Man?"

"Okay," I said hesitantly. I opened the door, and Mourat very slowly came in. He then handed me the bag of ice.

"Put that on it for twenty minutes, and it'll take the swelling down."

"Thank you."

"Little Man," he said thoughtfully, "you don't have to tell me what happened, but if you do want to . . . well, I am here if you want to chat."

"Thank you."

"Make sure you leave it on for twenty minutes, and then come downstairs . . . there are a lot of thirsty Persians waiting for you."

"Okay," I said with a slight smile. I could not really figure Mourat out. I still did not know whether to trust him or not, as he would do incredibly kind gestures and then try and keep me out of the loop with his gambling. Perhaps he was only kind to me because he was looking after his investment. I guess I will never know.

Once I returned downstairs, I immediately went to work. I went into automatic pilot as I worked throughout the day. I smiled when I had to, and it appeared that my celebrity had reached within all depths of the hotel. Everyone knew who I was, even though I did not always know who he or she was. However, from early on, I learned to know everyone because it profited me more. I always asked them how their business was going, if they had told me something about it. They all used to tell me about their own children, and I used to write down the name of their children so that I would remember should I serve them again. I used to write it on the tab list. Mourat loved the idea, and used it himself! However, throughout that day, I was just hoping that my parents would not ring. I could not believe that I was having such thoughts, but I knew that I could not lie. I would break down for sure on the phone, and that would have been the end of that. I hoped that I would speak to my mother on the next call anyway, and if that did happen, I would break down for sure.

I did not eat on that particular day. I had lots of tea and played one game of backgammon and served tea for the rest of the day until two o'clock in the morning. My parents did not ring me, and I was as happy as I was sad about that fact. I remember after the bar closed that night that I went to my usual seat on the back row of the lounge and stared at the television until I fell asleep. I did not want to go to bed, even though I was incredibly tired. I woke up at around three naturally and decided that I should retire, as I did not want to be found there first thing in the morning. I made my way up to my room, undressed, and got into my pajamas. I had no energy for oral cleansing, and so I picked up my family's photographs and fell asleep next to them. I cannot remember if I cried to sleep on that occasion, but if I did not, it was because I had no energy to cry, rather than me becoming stronger. I still slept with the lights on and the curtains drawn. The only aspect of living that I did get used to was the noises from outside. As tired as I was, I know that when I went to sleep I prayed to God that I would not remember what happened the day before. I knew it would not happen, but it did not stop me praying.

My father always said, "Tomorrow is a different day."

CHAPTER 11

The next two days that past were dark days for me. As hard as I could, the memory of that slap on the street was not leaving me the way that I had hoped it would. To add to that, my parents had not called me for three days straight, which I found very strange. The first night I had hoped that they wouldn't, because emotionally I did not think I would have handled it. However, now I was very much missing them and needed to hear their voices. I had decided that if they did not call by nine, my time, I would call them. I really hoped that they would call, because I did not want to anger my father for wasting money by calling them. I had only left the hotel once since that eventful afternoon to get some bread, cheese, yogurt, and water. I thought that I deserved a little cheese considering my new earnings and bad luck on the street. I had played three games of backgammon, and I still maintained my one hundred percent record. I have to say that Mourat's bets were no longer as large as they used to be, but that took pressure off me, and the bets were real. I continued to serve tea with considerable success, which was the one activity that really took my mind off all my problems. I now had a temporary second nickname. Due to my slightly bruised face, some of the hotel guests that were on friendly terms with me began to call me Rocky. I have to say that I was quite partial to that name, as Rocky was my hero! I had tried hard to get on with things as well as I knew how, yet the shock of that afternoon had really scared me.

I woke up on this particular day and made my way straight to the kitchen, because I wanted tea. Once I arrived at the kitchen, I found Mourat up and looking unusually alive. He was well dressed and had even bothered to apply after-shave. He strolled into the kitchen with a smile.

"Little Man, I have some good news for you."

"A pay rise?"

"Good try, but no," he said with his cheeky smile.

"Then what?"

"Someone has a letter today."

159

"Who me?"

"No, your auntie," he quipped sarcastically. "Of course you."

"Where? Where?" I asked enthusiastically.

"On my desk," he said as he followed me. I was already halfway there. As I approached the desk, I could see the red sign on the airmail envelope with the *Express* stamp on it. I ripped it open to find all the documentation that I had asked for, all held together with a paper clip. On top was a letter, and it was from my mother. I knew that, because I recognized her handwriting.

"Your documentation?" Mourat asked.

"Aha," I said half ignoring him as I took the letter and the documents to my little corner in the lobby to read. I was almost scared to read the letter. It had been so long since I had heard from my mother. This was the closest I had been to her since my departure. The fact that she had written that letter with her own hands, the fact that I recognized the paper as the type she always wrote on, the fact that she must have touched that paper, and best of all, the fact the letter still smelled like her made me so happy. The letter read:

To My Darling Abbas,

How are you, my sweet? You cannot imagine how I miss you, my boy. The house does not feel the same. I keep thinking that you are here or that I see you. I even think that I can hear you some afternoons playing with your friends outside. I go outside to see Suroosh, Farhad, Paiman, and the rest of them playing football. I search for you, but I can't see you. I have realized that my life is not the same without you, my darling. You were the soul of my life; you still are, and you always will be. I am sorry that I cannot speak to you on the telephone, but your father does not think it is healthy for either of us at the moment. However, he did promise me that we will speak soon. You do not know how proud of you I am, Abbas. You were my little boy only a few days ago, and now you are a man on your own. No one else could do what you are doing, my boy, but you can, because you are special. I cannot imagine how hard it must be for you. Just be strong a little longer, my darling. Pray to God, and you will see that He will answer you. I pray for you every night, Abbas, just as I taught you to. I will not tell you all the things that you have to do, because I know that you are a good boy and are doing them already. I know my boy. Just know that I am more sorry that I had to let you go at the airport than I am sorry about anything else in my life. I know that this might be a little hard for you to understand, but you will know what I saying soon. I am trying my hardest to join you, my child. If you are ever sad and think that life is hard, know that you are not alone, and that I am thinking of you. I love you more than life itself, my darling. If I could make myself go through the hardships instead of you, know that I would in a heartbeat . . . you are my flesh, you are my blood, and I love you more than anything else in the world. Whatever happens, know that I am really proud of you.

I love you, my darling son.

Your mother,

Marzieh

P.S. Mamanjoon sends her love and says that she misses you dearly.

I must have re-read that letter almost ten times. I had tears in my eyes as I read it every time. When I had been in Iran, I had always been embarrassed when my mother had shown me emotion, but now I was ashamed of myself for having been embarrassed when I was with her. I truly did not know what I had when I was with her. Now I would have done anything to see her and to tell her that I loved her. I was so happy and sad at the same time. I had almost lost faith in my parents, thinking that they did not care about me, and this letter really changed that for me. To read that someone was proud of me put a real smile on my face. At the same time, I wanted to cry because I was missing my mother more than anything else in the world. I would have happily done anything to see her. Mourat could see that I in an emotional mood, and to his credit, he remained in his seat and let me get on with it. I was happy that it was morning, because I still had plenty of time to get to the consulate. I just had to get changed into something smart. I decided to carry out an experiment on something that I had thought about quite a lot.

I returned to my room and dug out all of my clothes just to realize that I was almost out of clean clothes. I had to do some washing soon, but that was a problem for later. I managed to put a respectable outfit together and put it on in a hurry. Then I considered once more carrying out my experiment, and then decided to go for it. I was fed up of carrying all of my money on me and needed to find somewhere safe for it. The hotel room was the obvious place, and even though Mourat had a safe and was already carrying some money for me, I did not fully trust him. I had met the cleaning girl a few times. She was quite young and always paid special attention to me. She seemed very friendly and looked trustworthy, but I had to check for myself. I therefore put a $50 note on my bedside cabinet in plain sight. I also pinned a $50 note to the bottom side of my mattress from underneath the bed. My thinking behind this was that I only had $100 to lose, which was indeed a lot of money. However, it was better to lose one hundred than a thousand. I also knew that I could make that money up in four or five weeks depending on how many deliveries I had for Hector. I wanted to see if I could trust the cleaner. If she decided to steal the first fifty, I wanted to see if she would go looking for more money. I came out of my room and locked it carefully behind me.

I walked downstairs past a few guests who greeted me with their "Hey there Rocky!" or "Ah, isn't it a shame for a boy to be on his own" remarks. It surprised me that some people thought that just because I was young—I was also deaf. It didn't really bother me anymore; I was used to it by now. Besides, the advantages that it brought with it outweighed the disadvantages in my opinion. As soon as Mourat saw me, he knew I was going out.

"When will you be back?"

"I don't know," I replied with a cheerful smile. "I am going to the consulate."

"Oh, okay."

"Why?"

"Well it's just that I wanted to know if you'll be here for tea, and . . ."

"Have you got a match lined up?" I asked, having read his direction of dialogue.

"Yeah, kind of," he responded, "but it's not definite anyway."

"I should be back by the evening for sure."

"It's okay; we'll sort something out."

"Okay," I said, "I've got to go."

"*You* take care."

"Thanks."

I was about to go when Mourat called me back. "Little Man?"

"Yeah?"

"Good luck."

"Thanks," I said appreciating his words. "I'll see you later."

Once I was out, I realized that I had to walk on the main street to get to the bus stop. I had not thought about that, as I had been so excited about my letter and documents. It was early in the morning, and usually I would not have been scared to walk out at that time, but when the man had slapped me, it had been lunchtime. I knew that I had to do it, so I gritted my teeth and made my way toward the main road. Now I was in two minds as whether to keep my head down or to look up ahead. If I did the latter, I thought I might make myself more of a target, and therefore, I tried to settle for a compromise between the two. I think I must have looked silly with my head going up and down like a yo-yo. I made it unto the main road without any real incidents.

Once I made my way toward the main road, I noticed my heart beating faster. I was just nervous. Though I was pretty sure that nothing would happen, it was the first time walking past the spot where I had been hit. I decided the best way to deal with this was to walk briskly. I wanted to get to the consulate quickly anyway, because I knew that the wait was going to be long. Once again, I made it to the bus stop without getting myself into any trouble. I was quite relieved, and it made me feel better. It had put me in a good mood for what was to come. I don't know why, perhaps naiveté, I actually thought that there would be a major breakthrough at the consulate on that day. Just because I had my papers, I thought they would issue me with a visa.

I waited for the bus for about twenty minutes. I was getting quite impatient when I noticed a lady next to me. She could not have been more than twenty-six years old. Like most nations, we Persians can always tell our own. She was very beautiful, with long, thick black hair and deep brown eyes. She had all the marks of a Persian lady. The lady looked at me and thought twice about talking to me. Temptation obviously got the better of her, as after a few minutes she decided to speak.

"Excuse me?" she asked very politely, in her delicately toned voice.

"Me?" I asked quietly pointing to myself. I knew she was talking to me as she was speaking Farsi, and there was no other person waiting for a bus.

"Yes," she said with an elegant smile, "you. Are you Persian?"

"Yes."

"Oh good," she said almost relieved, "I'm here alone, and it's good to see other Persians."

"Yeah, I know what you mean." I don't think she understood, which was quite comprehendible.

"So where is your mother?"

"In Tehran."

"Oh, sorry," she said backing off a little, "so you're here with your father?"

"No, I'm alone."

She hesitated for a while as she thought she had misunderstood. "Sorry?"

"It's okay," I said like a seasoned professional. "I am alone without my parents, and I'm okay. Honest." She smiled at me, but I think she still thought I was pulling her leg.

"Really," I said, "I'm going to the British consulate. I'm waiting for the bus."

"Oh, thank God," she said with a sigh of relief, "so this is the right stop for the British Embassy?"

"Actually, it's the consulate;" I said as a matter of fact. "The embassy is in Ankara."

"Oh, right," she said almost in shock. "Yeah that's what I meant."

"It's okay," I said trying to make her feel better, "I made the same mistake."

There was a slight pause as she was getting her brain back into check.

"So does the bus stop outside the embassy?" She saw me look at her. "I mean consulate."

"Yeah," I said, "but listen, may I ask you a question?"

"Sure."

"Do you speak English?"

"Yes, a little anyway."

"Okay," I said to her, with my cheeky smile, "I'll make you a deal."

"What?"

"I'll take you to the consulate and show you how it all works, if you come up with me and translate for me."

"I don't see why not," she said. "So you know how to get a ticket and everything?"

"Aha," I murmured in my overconfident, know-it-all manner. "Do you have a 100 Lira note?"

"I think so."

"Then you don't need a ticket," I informed her. "Just put the money in the machine; it works like a ticket."

"It does?"

"Yup."

She was suitably impressed with my knowledge. She then looked at me, "So then, what's your name?"

"Abbas, but some people call me Rocky or Little Man."

"They do, huh?" she said smiling. "Well, I'll call you Abbas! I'm Tarineh."

"Nice to meet you."

"You too."

We did not wait for much longer until the bus eventually came. We got onto the bus, and sure enough, we used our bills instead of tickets. We sat next together on the bus and talked all the way. I told Tarineh my rough situation, because she was probably going to find out anyway if she was going to translate for me. The poor lady had been forced to leave the country by her parents and told to go and try for a British visa so that she could live with her auntie in London. She told me that she hoped to get a visa; otherwise, she would be forced to marry a Persian man that her auntie had found for her. She told me that she did not love him, and it would not be right. I felt really sorry for her, because she looked so sad. It made me realize that every person in Istanbul had a story. It also made me quite proud, because I was coping as well as an adult. The fact that Tarineh was a woman took away a little from my ego boost, because one tends to be sexist at such an age, especially coming from a country like Iran!

Luckily, I recognized the correct stop, and we got off the bus right outside the consulate. As we approached the gates, I noticed that one of the armed guards was the same as my previous visit. Immediately, he recognized me. I walked ahead of Tarineh who was searching the depths of her handbag for her passport. I didn't even show my passport; the guard just let me in without speaking one word. He waved me though. I waited for Tarineh inside the consulate grounds. Once she was allowed in, she walked along with me,

"Did you know them?"

"Kind of," I said. "We met on my last visit." I kept it short, because I did not want her to know that I had to cry like a baby to be allowed in!

"Oh," she simply said.

We walked silently up that magnificent drive toward the consulate door. I think Tarineh was taking it in, just as I did on my first visit. I did not say anything, as it was obvious that she was admiring it in the manner that I did. As we entered, we separated into the queues, one for men and one for women. I was tapped down as before and allowed to enter. I did not see Tarineh for a few minutes. As soon I was within the actual consulate, I went and took my number. It was not as busy this time. It seemed like I had an hour wait. I looked along the cubicles, and sure enough, my spectacled interviewer from the previous visit was there working at his usual counter. I noticed that he also clocked me and even gave me a little nod. From my previous visit, I knew that this little gesture was a highly animated course of communication for this somewhat anally retentive individual.

Eventually, Tarineh came through and sat next to me.

"They certainly search you properly, don't they?"

I just laughed, as I saw the naughty side of what she was saying. At first, she was shocked at my laughter, but after a few seconds of determining whether to be serious or take the joke, she laughed along with me.

"So what number do you have?" I asked. She showed me her ticket. "I think we have about twenty minutes between us."

"Will that be enough?"

"I don't know," I said feeling a little uneasy. "I hope so. If not, then you go and do you stuff."

"Okay."

We sat together for about forty minutes and talked about anything and everything. I was quite surprised about what Tarineh actually told me. She told me about her boyfriend back in Shiraz and how she almost married once, but the groom ran off with another woman. This was all very interesting to me, because a lot of things that my aunts had talked about to my mother now made a bit more sense. Marriage in Iran was a complicated business! Eventually, the number before mine flashed, and I was ready to go up with Tarineh. We waited for about five minutes before the next number flashed. It had, however, skipped my number. I did not know what to do. I got up to go and talk to someone when my spectacled friend started waving at me from his cubicle to sit down from his cubicle. He was seeing another person at the time, but it was obvious he knew what was going on.

"What happened?" Tarineh asked in a hushed voice.

"I think that man over there wants to see me," I said pointing to my friend.

"Okay."

Only a few minutes later, my number flashed up there, and of course, my spectacled friend's cubicle was empty. Tarineh and I walked to it, and the man smiled at me.

"You're back I see," he said to me. Tarineh began to translate, and to be fair to her, she was very good.

"I have brought the things you asked for," I said to the man and Tarineh simultaneously.

The man nodded with a smile and looked through the papers. After about five minutes of inspection, he looked back up. "Good," he said, "you've brought all that I asked for."

"Does that mean I can have my visa now?" Tarineh looked at me in a funny way before translating. Once the man heard what I said, he began to laugh.

"What?" I asked. I really did not see the humor in my statement.

"It's not quite easy," the man said still laughing. "You come back in exactly ten days at between two and three o'clock. It is important you come at the time that I have given you, because you will miss you appointment."

Once Tarineh translated for me, I looked at the man. "Thank you," I said in English. I felt quite hurt inside, as I did not like being laughed at. My over optimism had shown my age, and I looked a little stupid. This felt even worse, considering how I had portrayed myself in front of Tarineh. I took away a good lesson that day. The man took my papers and that was the end of my consulate visit.

Tarineh still had a good few numbers. "I'll wait for you, and we can go back together if you like," I offered.

"Are you sure?"

"Yeah."

"Thank you," she said smiling at me, "but you don't have to."

"No," I said, "I'll wait for you."

"Well, thank you."

I think she was quite touched that I was waiting in order to help her with the bus again. In fact, I was doing for myself too. I felt better traveling with someone else anyway. It was not going to make that much difference to me in terms of time. It served both of our purposes. Obviously, I did not inform her of my interest in this offer!

I sat there in silence and watched Tarineh take care of her business. She eventually came back and looked at me with the implication that she was ready to leave.

"Are you ready?" she asked.

"Yeah."

I stood up, and we walked out of the building without saying anything. Once we were on the drive, I looked up at her.

"So how did it go?"

"Well," she said with sad eyes, "at the moment, it looks like I'm marrying that guy."

"Why? What happened?"

"God knows," she sighed. "They want a million different papers."

"They did the same for me," I explained. "That's normal I think."

"I guess so."

Together we walked to the bus stop, and this time, Tarineh needed no help with the procedures. It was quite pleasing to see that she knew what to do because of me. We chatted a little on the bus, but it was obvious that her mind was somewhere else. What a difference an hour made. On our journey to the consulate, she could not stop speaking, and now she was forcing herself to say two words. It was obvious that she didn't want to marry this man and needed to get the visa through the proper channels. As I was finding out quicker and quicker, this was not an easy task.

We got off the bus next to the market place, opposite the road to where I had met Tarineh. As we were looking to cross the road, Tarineh reached and held my hand to help me over. I did not know what to say. I was quite insulted, and yet I was quite pleased all at the same time. We reached our initial meeting place, and there seemed to be an awkward silence. I did not really know Tarineh that well, but she seemed to be the most genuine person that I had met. She looked at me with her sad eyes; I was too embarrassed to look back at her.

"So then, Abbas," she said with her put on smile, "I guess that is it."

"Yeah."

"Will you be okay?"

"I have been so far," I murmured. "Will you be all right?"

"I think so," she uttered. "I have a few things to learn about this place yet, and you won't be around to show me."

I really wanted to tell her where my hotel was, and even though my instincts were telling me good things about this lady, it was against all that I had been taught. Having said what I did pretty much broke every other rule that I had been taught.

"It's not all that hard," I told her, "you'll be fine."

With that, she leaned over and kissed me on my cheeks. Then she spent a fair few seconds wiping off her lipstick off my cheeks. I think I must have turned extremely red!

"Good luck with everything, Tarineh," I whispered.

"You too, Abbas," she sighed, "you too."

She turned an was about to walk away when I called after her. "Tarineh?"

"Yeah?" she smiled on the turn.

"I hope you don't have to marry that man." She came up to me and stroked my cheek without saying anything and then left. I watched her disappear in the midst of the crowd. That was the last time I saw her. For a long time, I wondered what had happened to her. I wondered if she ever thought what had happened to me. I hoped that she did not have to marry that man. It was strange how someone touched me in such a short space of time and then continued on her own path. I think I had made an impact on her too. It was very strange, as we shared quite personal information, and yet we were strangers and completely different ages.

I stood there pensively thinking about what had happened and how I would never see Tarineh again. I then turned around and saw that I was near Hector's shop and thought about going in to see if he was satisfied with my work. I did not really want to go in, but if I did, I would know when my next delivery would be. Cautiously, I made my way to Hector's shop to find it empty. Suddenly, Hector emerged through his back door and came round to me with a huge smile.

"Abbas, my friend," he said, "great job yesterday."

"Thanks," I muttered. Before I knew it, Hector was hugging me and kissing me on each cheek. It was a little too much again and made me feel slightly uncomfortable.

"One minute," he said as he ran out back again. I assumed my position on the little stool and waited. Hector returned with a bottle of cold Fanta, which I really wanted. I was very thirsty after the day at the consulate.

"Thank you," I said. I took the bottle and downed the entire bottle. Hector watched me with his huge grin. He was not dressed as smartly as he usually was.

"I see you were thirsty, my friend."

"Yes," I said catching my breath, "I had not had a drink all day."

"Good."

There was a little pause as I decided on the best way to approach the subject. "Hector?"

"Yes?"

"I was just wondering," I said, "when will my next delivery be?"

"Ah," he said off guard, "I should think about three days."

"Okay," I uttered, "I will be back in three days."

"That would be great."

"Thank you for the Fanta."

"My pleasure," he said smiling. "Oh, by the way?"

"Yes?" I asked on the turn.

"Do you want me to swap your $10 note?"

"Eh," I stuttered, "no . . . no thanks. It's at home, and I didn't know I was coming here today. I will bring it as planned when I come for the next delivery."

"As you please."

"Thank you, though."

He waved at me as if to indicate it was nothing. I actually did have the $10 note with me, but I did not want to show Hector the rest of my money, as it was all together. I thought that it wasn't a good idea to show people where I kept my money.

So once again, with my mind all over the place, I began to make my way back to the hotel. I had forgotten all about the money that I had left out and the money that I had hidden. I started to think that I had done the wrong thing. Maybe the cleaner would not find the extra $50 under the bed, but she would certainly see the one on the bedside table. I was beginning to wonder why I had done such a thing in the first place. Technically, I was asking someone to steal $50 from me. I began to get angry with myself, and the frustration showed in my walking pattern. I was walking extremely quickly, almost too quickly. I had now forgotten all about the incident in the street only a few days prior, because my head was taken up with an extra problem that I had created for myself. Unfortunate things that happened to me only made me sad, but self-inflicted incidents made me angry as well. If the money was gone, I could never tell my father. He had always made a point of me looking after my things. He also made me promise to look after the money with my life. This was hardly doing that, even though at the time I was thinking that I was being clever.

As I walked, I began to have a flashback of one of the only times when my father had beaten me. I was only six years old, and I had a new bike. I had loaned the bike against a tree, and I had climbed the tall tree all the way to the top. My father had been walking past, and he shouted up to me to make sure that no one took the bike while I was climbing. Caring very little for his comment, I waved away the remark that someone would actually take away my bicycle. Thirty minutes or so later, I climbed down to see that this very thing had happened. I returned home with my tail between my legs, apologizing profusely. It was not enough though. My father went into a rage that I will not forget until the day I die. He picked me up with one hand and literally threw me across the room where I hit the wall. Without hesitation, he undid his belt and began to beat me with all his might. My uncle was there day, and if he had not pulled my father away from me, I really think that he would have done some serious damage. In a very similar way as when the man had slapped me, I only cried after the incident was over.　The shock did not really allow me to feel the pain until it was finished. I wondered if I was happy to be in Istanbul because I could try to hide the fact that I lost $50, if in fact that did happen. My father used to tell me that a real man should know the value of money. With all these thoughts circulating around my head, I was back at the hotel before I knew it. Even though I was thirsty and needed more bread and water, I had to go to my room first and see what had happened to the money.

I entered the lobby to find Mourat on the phone. He tried to stop me with his hands, but I indicated that I would be back soon. Pretending that I needed the toilet urgently, I ran up the smelly stairs. I actually continued my run all the way to my room and unlocked it with in one smooth movement. As I entered the room, I immediately saw the $50 on the bedside table where I had left it. The only thing that was different was that the hotel room ashtray was on top of it in order to stop it from flying away. One could not imagine my happiness. I was so relieved. For the previous thirty minutes, it had become the most important thing to me, and now it was all okay. Though I was still sure that the other fifty was still pinned on the bottom of the mattress, I bent down and checked. Sure enough, everything was intact.

I sat on my bed and smirked to myself and thought about getting some provisions. As I was about to leave, I had a second thought. If the money was still there, did that mean that the room was safe or were they trying to trick me into leaving more money? With that thought, I decided to play further. I did not know why, because only thirty minutes before I was worried about losing the little that I had left. Now I was actually going to hide some money around the room to see what happened. I slid open my cupboard and took out a pair of shoes that I owned. I then took out the sole in the left shoe and then put the sole back over it. I put the shoes to the back of the cupboard and covered them with clothes. I then decided to use a trick that I had seen a Bollywood film. I had some blue tack, and with that, I put two $100 bills on the upside of the bedside cabinet drawer. So if someone opened it, it looked like it was empty. The bottom of the cupboard only had a slight gap, barely big enough for my hands. By this, I mean the space between the bottom of the cupboard and the floor. The cupboard was also very heavy. So I blue-tacked two bills to the bottom of the cupboard as far back as I could reach. Right there and then, I decided that it was too stupid to carry all of my money all in one pocket. So split the money all around my body. I only kept one hundred in my trouser pockets. The rest were split between my pants and my socks. The majority, however, remained in my pants, and that is where it continued to remain for the rest of my stay.

On my way back from the corner shop, I saw a small boy with a portable shoe cleaning kit. I had seen many of these children in Istanbul as I had walked about in the market place. They charged one hundred Liras and cleaned the shoes while their customers stood there. They sat on little stools, usually against a wall with their toolboxes and cleaning kits in front of them. There was a foothold on the box that carried all the equipment for the clients to rest their feet, while the children cleaned their shoes. While sipping my water, this gave me a small idea, but I decided to keep it to myself for a while.

Once I returned, I checked the money again. It was obvious that it was still going to be there, but I had only gone out for about fifteen minutes. I ate by myself, and as lonely as it was, my mood was nothing like it had been at previous meal times. I still looked at my family pictures and missed them all dearly. The reality was gradually beginning to sink in that it was going to be likely that I would not see them for a long time. I could not but help being optimistic about my mother joining me though. I never gave up hope on her, because I knew that she would never give up hope on me. It was impossible for my father to leave Iran, which of course meant that my only hope was my mother.

After dinner, I strolled down the stairs and immediately got to work on the tea and the bar. I was getting quite familiar with all the spirits too. I only really got confused with mixers for drinks, but only Westerners really ordered them. However, there were only a handful of Westerners that ever stayed there. I didn't like them as much, because they were meaner with their tips. The few English people that I had met there in Istanbul had not left a great impression on me, but I could not help but to judge a whole nation on the very few people that I had met. I was beginning to get a very cynical opinion of people in general. That particular night, it was quiet, and on quiet shifts, I used to do a lot of thinking. I used to try and look at people and guess if they were good people just by their faces. I learned a lot from the way they acted and the way they looked at other people. I was behind the bar when I saw Mourat move through with his knowing smile. I hated it when he used to do that. As soon as he saw me, he made a gesture like a telephone. Then he about turned and went to his thrown. I jumped to my feet with great excitement and ran to my usual booth. I closed the door behind me and took a deep breath. I just hoped and prayed that I would hear my mother's voice.

"Hello?"

"Abbas?" my father's voice echoed down the rusty line.

"Oh," I sighed, "hi."

"How are you?"

"Is Maman there?"

"She is asleep."

"When can I speak to her?" I asked almost crying. "I promise not upset her, Baba."

"I know, my son," he said. "I promise you, and I have never broken a promise to you, right?"

After a brief pause, "Right."

"Well, I promise," he went on, "that the next time I call you'll speak to her."

"Okay."

"So how are you?"

"I'm okay," I said. "I got the documents this morning."

"You did?" he shouted excitedly. "I was going to ask."

"Yeah, they came all intact, and I got the letter from Maman."

"Good."

"Thank her for me, please."

"She says thanks too. She got two letters from you today."

"They came?" I asked excitedly. This completely changed my mood. I had wondered if they got there.

"So this is what I want you to do, Abbas," my father went on in a slightly more serious tone. "Tomorrow I want you to go back to the consulate with all the documents and . . ."

"Baba?" I tried to cut in.

"Go with the documents, and . . ." he tried to speak over me.

"Baba?" I said louder.

"What is it?" he snapped. "I'm trying to tell you what to do."

"I know," I responded in a hushed voice.

"Then what is it?"

"It's just that . . ."

"What? Spit it out, boy."

"Well, it's just that I have already been to the consulate."

"I know, but you have to go again with the documents."

"I have."

"When?"

"Today."

"How could you have?" he asked. "You said that you got them today."

"I did," I proclaimed, "this morning. I immediately got changed and went there."

"You did what?" he asked. "Why didn't you wait for me to tell you what to do?"

"Well, because I knew what to do," I said quietly. I was afraid that he was going to shout again. "The man at the consulate said that I should go back when I have the documents."

"That's true, but you should have waited for me to call in case I had some instructions for you."

"I know, Baba," I said, "but you had not called for several days, and I didn't know if you were going to call again soon. I just want to get this done quickly so that I can get out of this . . ." I paused there, as I knew that I was speaking too much, and I did not want to upset my father.

"This what?" he asked in a hushed voice.

I didn't answer the question, and a slight silence filled there air as my father considered his next question. "This what, Abbas?"

"Nothing, Baba," I said, "it's just that you said yourself that I don't know how long this money will last, so I tried to get things done quicker."

He thought about what I had said, and he could not really argue. He also had a point, maybe there was something that I needed to know but I had not thought about that.

"It's okay, Abs," he said, "you did what you thought was best. No, you did well actually. You took initiative, and that is great to see,

Abbas."

"Thank you," I said, halfway smiling. I don't know if my father suddenly understood that he was dealing with a child, or he actually thought I had done well. Nevertheless, it was amazing to hear such words from his mouth.

"So what happened?"

"Well," I said much more enthusiastically, "I saw the same man, and he told me that I had all the documents that he had asked for, which he was pleased about."

"He was?"

"I think so," I went on, "and he told me that I should go back in ten days exactly between two and three o'clock."

"He did?"

"Yeah," I said, "what does that mean, Baba?"

"I don't know, Son," he said, "but let us hope it is good."

"I'll pray for something good," I said.

"You do that, Son," he said thoughtfully. "Now you be good, and I will call you again soon, before you go back to the consulate."

"When will you call, Baba?"

"I don't know, Abbas, but soon," he muttered. "Now you only go out when you have to."

"I know."

"Good-bye then, Abs."

"Baba?"

"Yes?"

"You won't forget your promise, will you?"

"No, Son—no, I won't."

"Thank you."

"My pleasure,' he said, "now you go to bed."

"Okay, Baba."

So what if I didn't go to be straight away and stayed up? The way I thought about it was that as long as I did not go out at night, it would not matter. Besides, I was earning money, which my father would always approve of—well, the tea job anyway. I'm not sure if he would have approved it, but the fact that I was trying might have made him happy.

That conversation had been the best that I had with my father since I had arrived in Istanbul. It was also the first conversation that I had when I did not cry. That really put me in a good mood for the rest of the evening. Even though it was quiet, I enjoyed the rest of my shift and went to bed at a fairly reasonable hour.

When I came into my room, I realized that I had no more clothes to wear for the following day. I was dreading the inevitable. I had to clean my clothes. I took all my dirty clothes into the bathroom and turned on the shower. As I watched the water onto them, I realized that I had no detergent. I pondered for a few minutes, and then decided that I was going to use soap. I wetted my clothes individually and then scrubbed the bar of soap across them. Then I rubbed the clothes together and tried to rinse them out. There was dirty water coming out of them so I presumed that I was cleaning them. I don't think that I did a terribly great job, but it seemed to be okay. I then tried to hang the clothes on objects around the bathroom in order for them to dry. I knew it would take time, because the room was already damp. I did not see any other way round the problem though.

I still slept with the lights on, and I might have even spilled a few tears as I looked at my family photographs, but in I was feeling emotionally better because my father had approved something that I had done. The thoughts of that man hitting me popped into my head once in a while, but it didn't get me down as it had done earlier in the day. It was surprising how a few encouraging words from my loved ones made such a difference.

CHAPTER 12

Five days passed, and I continued my life with as much routine as possible. I had done one more delivery for Hector. On that trip, there were no problems. I had not been followed, and Hector had given me a new $10 bill, plus my money for the new drop. Apart from getting food, that had been the only time I had left the hotel.

Even though I was beginning to cry less and get on with things without as much self-sorrow, on this one morning, I awoke feeling miserable. There was good reason for my sadness; if there was day that I needed my family with me, it was this one. I lay in bed and waited for the sun to rise properly. As I lay silently, I began to reminisce about my first night in that very same room. All the noises were highlighted, the sounds of the dripping taps, the noises from the random punters that made their way on the street down below, and the insects that cohabited my room with me. I managed to get a few more hours of sleep before I woke again at around eight.

I walked down the stairs in my customary manner to find Mourat halfway asleep as usual. I had not written a letter home since my last conversation with my father, five days prior. I walked straight to Mourat's desk, and after a half-hearted wave, I helped myself to some writing paper and a pen.

"Help yourself," he quipped. "Why don't you?"

"Thanks," I said cheekily. He showed me a little smile before dozing back off to sleep. I now had the free run of the hotel, and I felt comfortable with it too. I did work very hard though, and I knew that I had certainly bettered business for Mourat since my instruction as the tea boy. I slipped into my usual spot in the grotty old sofa and thought hard about what to write. It took me some time before I actually wrote anything, but once I started, I kept going.

Dear Maman,

How are you? I am doing well. In five days, I am to go back to the consulate. I gave them all of my documents, and they are looking at them. I think that is what they are doing anyway. I have learned how to make the time pass during the days, but I never stop thinking of you. I really miss you, Maman. Today I am eight, and no one here knows. It is the first birthday that I have had without you or my friends. I remember you telling me how lucky I was when I did not like one of my presents a few years ago. I know that now. I don't want any presents this year, I just want to see you. Baba promised that the next time he calls that we can speak to each other. I can't wait. It has been a long time since he rang. I have not heard from him in five days. I woke up early this morning wondering if you would call me today. I hope so! I don't mind if you don't, Maman. I had forgotten that you have nothing back in Tehran. When we left for the airport the house was empty. You'll join me soon anyway, so you don't have to put up with that much longer. I'm sure Baba will sort everything out and buy more things. He always seems to manage somehow.

If you and Baba had left Iran before the revolution, when we were rich, maybe we would all be together right now. I do a lot of thinking here. I have a lot of time to myself. In Tehran, I was always out playing football or on my bike. Here I have no friends, so instead I think. My money is lasting well. I am eating only once a day and not spending money on anything silly. Everyone here knows me now. Most people here are Iranian, and I am almost famous among them. Most of them are really good to me. One of the ladies who was staying here really looked like you. I didn't speak to her, though. She only stayed one or two days. I guess I had better go now, but I am thinking of you Maman, especially today. A birthday is not the same without you.

Lots of love,

Your son, Abbas

I folded the paper over and walked to the reception area and sealed it in an envelope. I wrote the address on the envelope very quietly in order not to wake up Mourat when he startled me with, "It's okay, I'm awake."

"You are?"

"I have been for a while," he yawned. "I just like to rest my eyes."

"I see."

There was a little pause as I played with my letter. It must have been obvious that I had something on my chest and wanted to speak to

Mourat.

"What is it?" he asked. "Spill it out."

"Nothing—well, actually there is something . . ."

He cut my line short with, "No, you can't have a pay rise."

"No, it's not that."

"Then what is it?" he inquired.

"Well, I was just wondering . . . ?"

"What?" he asked. He was quite curious now.

"You know those children that clean shoes on the street?"

"Yeah?"

"I was thinking that I could do that."

"I don't recommend it," he said very plainly.

"Why?" I asked almost disappointed.

"You shouldn't go on the streets," he said knowingly. "Those children are part of gangs, and if you try and do it too, you'll get hurt."

"Oh," I sighed, "but I didn't want to go on the street."

"So how could you work?"

"I was thinking that we could do it here."

"We? Here?" he asked rhetorically.

"Yeah," I went on more enthusiastically, "why not? Everyone here is either on business or trying to get visas."

"And?"

"Well, they all have to look smart," I explained. "We could have the box here in the lobby, and in the morning, if their shoes need a polish, they could get it done on the way to the embassies or their meetings."

"You've been thinking again, huh?"

"Also, we can do it like the Hilton in Tehran. My father told me that when he used to stay there, they used to polish shoes in the night and leave it outside the door for you."

" He did, did he?" he asked sarcastically.

"Yeah," I said smiling, "and guess what?"

"We could charge more for that!"

"You crack me up," he said laughing loudly.

"So?"

"So what?"

"So what do you think?" I asked imposingly.

"Well," he said stuttering, "I don't know. Have you not got enough jobs here?"

"I still have time."

"So if, and that is a big if," he protested, "I say yes to this crazy idea, how do we do this?"

"Well I was thinking . . ."

"Oh, no," he said sarcastically again. "I don't like it when you think."

"Very funny," I went on, "I was thinking that if you buy the equipment, which by the way I have seen in the market, we would go fifty-fifty."

"How does that work?" he asked. "I'll be the one paying for the equipment."

"Yes," I said, "but the idea is mine, and I will be doing the work too."

"Yes, but you'll be using my lobby," he argued.

"That is why you're getting fifty percent, for the money to buy the equipment and the use of your lobby."

"You're being clever again, and I don't like it when you're clever."

I just smiled at him, only for him to carry on. "So what happens when you leave?"

"Who will serve tea when I leave?"

"Someone else."

"Well, there you go."

He knew I had a good idea, because he had very low overhead on this particular venture. By cleaning fifty or sixty pairs of shoes, he would make his money back. As I was getting half of the money, it would take double the amount of shoes to make the money. After that, he would always be making profit. He also knew that not many other cheap hotels offered the same service.

"Okay," he said, 'I'll see what I can do."

"Cool," I screamed, "and you can't do anything bad, because I take the money and I give you your half."

"You're something else."

"I know," I said with my cheeky smile. "Oh, and Mourat?"

"What now?"

"Get a good box and a stool."

"Okay, go away now," he said, "you're getting cheeky!"

Happily, I walked off to the kitchen to get my morning glass of tea. This was a great result as I had expected Mourat to at least put up a fight on the percentage, but it was easier than I thought. I had therefore managed to get my fourth job in half as many weeks. I was pretty happy with myself. It made me feel slightly better and gave my birthday a good start.

The day was pretty eventless. I played a few games of backgammon with Mourat just for sport and served a few glasses of tea, but it was not until the night when things got a little more interesting. I had not seen Mourat since four o'clock, and I had been working behind the bar in the television lounge. The later it got, the more upset I became, as my parents still had not called me. The lounge was filling up fast, and I was getting quite busy. All the Persians were there ordering their usual drinks, and the tips were pretty good too. My parents, however, monopolized my thoughts, and nothing on that night was going to take that away. Suddenly, Mourat flew into the lounge and waved at me to go to him. I indicated that I was really busy and could not leave the bar immediately. He kept insisting and told me that it was important. For a split second, I thought that I had a phone call and dropped everything in my hands and ran to him.

"I have a surprise for you, Little Man."

"What?" I asked. "Do I have a call?"

"No," he said half shocked, "why? Are you expecting one?"

"I guess."

"We continued to walk into the lobby as Mourat carried on talking. "This, Little Man, is better than any call."

"I doubt it."

"No," he said, "you just wait and see."

With that, he revealed a really large and glamorous shoe cleaning box and stool. It had golden metal handles with beautifully constructed wooden frame and drawers. It came with all the supplies and a little stool covered with purple velvet. It was really beautiful, and I should have been more impressed than I showed.

"What?" he asked. "I thought this is what you asked for."

"It is," I said half-heartedly.

"It's one of the best ones out there," he carried on. "My friend gave it to me for a good price."

"Good."

"You don't like it?"

"No," I said, "it's really nice. We'll do great with it."

"That's what I like to hear," he said proudly. "Go and try it out."

I walked round the back of it and sat on the little stool against the wall near the entrance to the lobby. Actually, it felt quite comfortable. I started to look through all the little drawers and the compartments of the box. Mourat suddenly put his foot on the box with his smile.

"Let's see how good you are then, Little Man."

I looked up at him and did not say anything. I really did not want to clean his shoe for two reasons. First, he was not paying, but more importantly, the first pair of shoes that I cleaned signified an all time low for me. My parents had once been in the aristocracy, and though I was brought up in the lower middle classes, I was always told to behave as if I had been an aristocrat. This had been all my idea, and I had no room to complain, but I did not think that I would feel this bad when it came down to it. I took out the brown polish and the brush and began to smear it all over his shoe. Then with the shining cloth, I began to put my back into it. Mourat stood there observing with admiration. I was not going to allow Mourat know that I was upset, because it would have made me look weak. I wanted him to feel that I was comfortable with what I was doing, and thus did not have any complexes. I still believed that I could make some money from this, but I did not really want to be the one shining the shoes! It was too late now, and I had to do it.

After about five minutes, I did both of his shoes. He did not say anything at first while he inspected his shoes, so that he can give me his expert opinion. He then looked at me with his usual cocky smile and said, "Not bad at all. You just need to be a bit quicker."

"I thought I was quick."

"Yes," he said, "but you need to be quicker."

Then he started to whistle as he walked off into the kitchen. I sat there alone in the lobby and stared at the reception. I remembered once again that it was my birthday, and that my parents had not called me. I wanted to cry. I did not know for how long I had to continue living like this. I was trying to make the most of this experience, but it was still having its affects upon me in a major way. As I stared, suddenly, I felt a thud on my box. It was one of the Persian guests that had been there for a little while. I forget his name, but he always tipped me well when I served him tea.

"Can you do mine?" he asked.

"Sure."

I began to work, and he watched me in silence as I went about my work. I tried hard to be quicker than when I cleaned Mourat's shoes. The gentleman was pleased with my work and paid me my 100 Liras plus a tip. Of course, I put the tip in my own pocket and put the hundred in one of the drawers that I had decided to use as a till.

For the rest of the evening, I went to and fro from the kitchen to the bar and back to my box. A lot of people were having their shoes cleaned that night just because of the novelty value I think. Mourat had put up a sign for an overnight shoe cleaning service in the reception area. For that, he wanted to charge 250 Liras. I thought it was too much, but I did not care enough to say anything. There were some new guests in the hotel that day. It was a Persian family, and they had a little boy who was about my age. I had heard him earlier in the day crying because his mother had not bought him the chocolate that he had wanted. I had laughed at that incident privately, because I knew that I might have done the same not too long ago. I sat at the box counting the money we had taken in so far when the boy approached me with a 100 Lira note and put his foot on the box. This, for me, was the ultimate humiliation. I had not minded cleaning the shoes of people who were older than me, but I found it extremely difficult to cope with this. I hated the idea that someone else was thinking that they were better than me, especially when they were the same age as me, and in my opinion, not as intelligent. Maybe I had a superiority complex, or maybe that is the way the child psyche works. Nevertheless, I was very upset at having to clean this child's shoes. I picked up the brush and began to dip it into the polish.

As I was about to apply the polish to the child's shoes, Mourat called me from reception. "Hey, Little Man?"

"Yeah?"

"Phone call for you."

Without even looking at my customer, I dropped everything in my hands and ran to the booth. I closed the door and picked up the phone. "Hello?"

"My darling baby," my mother said. "Happy birthday, Sweetness." Her voice was so soft and gentle, and I could feel her love for me through every syllable that came out of her mouth.

"Maman?"

"What is it, Baby?"

"I miss you so much," I sobbed. Tears were flowing freely down my cheeks, but I was happy. Hearing my mother's voice just brought all the emotions out of me.

"I miss you too, my darling," she said. "It's just not the same here without you."

"Really?"

"Of course, my darling," she sobbed. "What do you think?"

"I don't know," I said. "Sometimes I thought that you'd forgotten about me. I thought Baba might call more."

"He wants to but . . ." She paused, but I knew why, my father must have been next to her.

"Baba is there, isn't he?"

"Yes."

"Is it because we can't afford to speak too often?"

"Yes, Abbas," she said, "that is the only reason."

"Are you crying, Maman?"

"No baby," she said trying to hide her sadness. "I'm not."

"Don't cry, Maman," I said trying to be strong for her. "I'm fine here. I can take care of myself. Don't worry about me. I am doing really well."

"I know, Sweetness," she said. "We are so proud of you—we all are."

"You are?"

"Of course," she said almost in shock, "do you think any boy could do what you are doing?"

"I don't know," I said plainly.

"Well, they can't," she said firmly, "even if you didn't do as well as you are doing, I'd be proud of you."

"Thank you."

"Abbas?"

"Yes?"

"I'm so sorry that I can't be there for your birthday. I know it must be lonely for you."

"Don't worry, Maman," I said. "I'm fine. I got my birthday present by speaking to you."

"My baby . . ."

"Maman, it's okay," I said trying to comfort her. "I also have your letter that you sent with the papers."

"Baba told me you liked it."

"I loved it," I said, "send me more if you like."

"You know I will."

I was trying so hard not to cry any longer, but I remembered my promise to my father. I would have done anything to be with my mother at that time. I was so sad and happy at the same time. It was so good to hear her voice again, but at the same time, it made me realize how much I missed her. I had missed that kind of attention, especially in a time when I had really needed it.

"Does Baba want to speak to me?"

"Yes, he does, my darling," she said, "but before I forget, Mamanjoon sends her love."

"Say hi for me."

"I will."

"Go, Maman. I'll be fine," I said. "I don't want the bill to get too big."

"Okay, Baby. I love you."

"I love you too, Maman."

There was a slight pause as my father took the receiver from my mother. I knew that I had to recompose myself in order to give the impression that I was in total control.

"Abbas?"

"Hi, Baba," I replied in my merriest tone.

"How are you, my boy?"

"Good, thank you, and you?"

"Can't complain," he said with gentle humor. "Happy birthday."

"Thank you, Baba."

"You're a man now, huh?"

"I guess."

"If you like, you can buy yourself some chocolate or something," he said. "Sorry that we can't be there or give you presents."

"It's okay, Baba," I responded. "I don't want chocolate anyway. Besides, it's dark outside, and I don't want to leave the hotel."

"Good boy," he said, "but if you want chocolate tomorrow, it will still be okay."

"Thank you, Baba, but I don't think I will."

"So?" he asked, "what are you doing tonight?"

"Oh, nothing," I said as I looked at my dirty hands. "I'll probably watch some television."

"Good for you, Son."

"You go now, Baba," I said. "It's late over there."

"Okay, Abbas," he sighed. "You take care of yourself, and I'll call you the night of your consulate trip."

"Okay."

The phone clicked, and I knew that there would be another five days before I spoke to either of them again. Five days was a long time for me then. I had already managed to survive five days before, maybe it would be easier this time round. A plus was that I knew for sure that they would ring on the fifth day on this occasion. I sat there for a few minutes making sure that there were no signs of my tears as there were people in the lobby, one of which was the boy who was still waiting for me.

I came out of my booth and saw the boy still standing next to the box.

"Sorry," I said very plainly and got back to the task at hand. I was still uncomfortable about cleaning the boy's shoes, but at least I had got to speak to my mother. That had given me real strength, and I was more prepared to get my hands dirty. The fact that she had said that they were all proud of me made feel on top of the world. Those were the opinions that mattered to me. I knew perfectly well that I did not have to listen to anyone, but I was always bothered by what my parents had to say. Their approval meant the world to me. I was in my own world, thinking about how my father had become a little mellower during this conversation.

"What is your name?" the boy asked.

I looked up at him, and quite honestly, I did not want to speak to him. I just wasn't in the mood. I knew, however, that I had to. "Abbas." I told him what he wanted to know and returned to my work, hoping that would be the end of the conversation.

"Do you not want to know what my name is?" he asked.

I didn't, but I couldn't say that. "Sure."

"Amir," he said, "my name is Amir."

"Hi," I said.

"Hi," he replied, "we're here to get a visa for America. I can't wait until we go there. My father says they have amazing toys."

Now I knew what Mourat was talking about when he said that I had to learn to clean faster. It was only for my own sake. I had not talked to a child for a long time, and my patience was running out with this one.

The rest of the night was very busy with me predominantly working in the television lounge serving drinks. I finished very late that night. Usually, I might have stayed downstairs and sat in front of the television until I began to doze off. However, on that night, I was ready to go to my room. As happy as I had been to hear my mother's voice, it was no ordinary birthday. Immediately, I went and checked that my money was still where I had hid it. Then I slowly sat myself on the edge of the bed and stared at my family's picture. It was a repetitive act, but I did not get bored with it. Eventually, I lay on the bed and continued to stare blankly at the pictures. I cannot remember what I was thinking, but I know that I did not cry. I just fell asleep.

CHAPTER 13

During the next five days, I tried to occupy myself with as much work as I possibly could. The only major incident that was worth reporting was that I lost my first game of backgammon. It was tight, but I was outplayed by a better player. Luckily, Mourat did not put a lot of money on me, as he knew that I was the weaker player. I think he just hoped for a miracle. I did not really feel that bad for him, because he had not lost that much money. The shoe-cleaning business was doing very well, and Mourat kept commenting on how it had all been his idea. He used to do it to annoy me! In response to his comments, I always used to point out that he had to trust me to give him his fair share of the money. He always used to smile at me knowingly. He never tried to check whether I was trying to steal from him. Maybe he had learned his lesson before. It was very tempting, but I could never bring myself to touch anything that was not mine. Besides, I did not share the tips with him, so I always made more than him anyway. During those five days, I was not on top form, because my birthday was still in the back of my mind. Having heard my mother's voice, too, had been a reminder of what I was missing by being in Istanbul. I had no choice but to keep myself occupied with as much work as I could find.

The day came that I had to go to the consulate. I came downstairs in my smart clothes and gave my own shoes a cleaning. I was smiling to myself, because I could do something for free. The same way I could drink free tea, I could clean my shoes for free. It was the little things that seemed to entertain me. Mourat walked into the lobby with a self-gratifying smile.

"Morning, Little Man."

"Morning."

I did not know why, but I had decided to take another risk on this day.

"Mourat, do you have some of the Liras I asked you to put in the safe for me?"

"I have all of it," he said with a smile. "Do you want it?"

"Yes, please."

Without hesitation, he opened the safe, and there, as he had left it, was my pile. It had built up slightly as I had added some tips to it. I took the Liras, and then as Mourat was about to shut the safe I stopped him.

"Mourat?"

"Yes?"

"Can you put some of my dollars in there?"

"Sure," he said, "how much?"

"Around $800," I said softly. I did not know how he would respond. He very coolly looked at me and winked.

"No problem, Little Man."

I took out my dollars and counted out $800 in front of him. He took it, put it in an envelope, and wrote my name on it. Then he put it back in the safe where my Turkish Liras had been. I did not know whether I was doing the right thing, but I just did not want to worry about losing the money anymore. I also had four or five hundred hidden in my room.

"Thank you, Mourat."

With that, I began to walk off to the kitchen to get myself some tea before my trip to the consulate.

"No problem, Little Man," Mourat said, as I was disappearing round the corner. "Oh, by the way . . ."

"I turned to see what he was going to say. "Yeah?"

"Are you going to write a letter today?"

"No," I said, "I will speak to my parents tonight."

He had actually started to get on my case because I had stopped writing as many letters as I used to. It was nice of him to do that, I think. He said that it was important to write letters to your parents. Mourat's own parents lived in a village a long way away from Istanbul, and he had told me that ever since I had arrived, he had started to write letters to them too. I went to the kitchen and pensively poured myself a glass of tea. I sipped at it and thought about my day ahead. I wondered what was going to happen at the consulate. I hoped that I would be as lucky as my last two previous visits in finding someone to translate for me. I wondered if I would see Tarineh there. I knew that the likeliness would not be high, but it was certainly possible. It had been ten days since she was told to get her papers.

I walked off the bus outside the consulate and walked to the gates. The armed guards both recognized me, as they were the original two from my first visit. With gentle smiles, they opened the gates without even looking at my passport. I walked up the gravelly drive through the meticulous gardens of the consulate. As I reached the doors, I was greeted by the gentleman in charge of searches. Once through, I went straight for the ticket machine. It was a really busy day at the consulate. I could not even see a free seat. I knew that I was going to have to wait for a long time. As soon as I saw the crowds, I was less worried about finding a translator as I was about how long it would take to be seen.

As I reached toward the ticket machine to take a number, a series of loud taps stopped me on my way. They were coming from the booth of my spectacled friend. He had recognized me and was waving at me like a crazy baboon. I did not understand what he wanted me to do, so I looked at him harder. He began to point to the side that was at the front of the consulate next to the glass booths. This, however, was only a door that the consulate staff ever used. On my previous visits, I had not witnessed anyone but the staff to go through that door, and for that reason, I was hesitated going to it. The man kept signaling toward the door, and so I started to walk very unsurely toward it. As I did, I saw the man smile from behind his glass booth. The more he smiled, the faster I walked.

As I reached the door, I could no longer see my spectacled friend as the angle was too acute. I stood there waiting for what seemed like hours. In fact, it was minutes, but I was still unsure as to what I was doing. Doubts were going through my mind as if this is what the man had wanted me to do. If it was, why had he wanted me to do this? These thoughts were worsened by the fact that almost everyone in the consulate was staring at me and obviously whispering about my under their breath. I was now panicking a little, because if the man wanted me to go through the door, then I would not have anyone to translate for me. I did not want to approach people, because they were all talking about me and probably judging me on the way that I had acted so far, the clothes that I was wearing, and of course, the fact that I was alone.

Suddenly, the door opened, and the spectacled man opened the door. He guided me in with a mere hand gesture. I felt very strange walking on the other side of the door. It felt good, because I felt a little different to everyone else. I had been allowed on the side that no one else usually is. Behind the booths was an open plan office with computers and photocopying machines. The desks were all immaculate, and the people working there were dressed in beautifully made business attire. The carpet looked soft and fresh and seemed like it had only been shampooed the day before. There was a rosy smell of air freshener, which contrasted to the pungent odors of an overcrowded room. The air conditioning seemed like the icing on the cake. It was quite awesome.

I followed the man through another door at the back of that office, which led to a long corridor. This corridor had polished floorboards instead of carpet on the ground. There was a heavy oak bench outside of some grand oak doors in the center of the corridor. At the far end, I could see an opening that resembled a foyer, also a grand scale. The man indicated that I should sit on the bench and wait. He talked, too, but I only understood the hand gestures. I sat there gazing hard at all the details that this marvelous building had to offer. There were huge paintings hanging on either side of the wooden doors. They were of horses and foxes; now I know that they were about hunting back in England. These oil paintings looked like nothing I had seen before. They were so large; they were bigger than me.

I must have waited there for over one hour. I did not see anyone for the duration of that one hour, and I was beginning to panic that they had forgotten about me. Suddenly, I saw a man who looked very Persian walk toward me. He smiled at me, but did not say anything. I smiled back at him and also stayed muted.

The man knocked on the door and a loud, deep voice immediately responded. "Enter."

The man went in, and once again, I was alone. I waited for another fifteen minutes, and I think I was about to go and try to find my friend when the door opened. A man of considerable stature and class stood before me. Immediately, I rose to my feet. The man, dressed in a finely tailored beige suit, salmon pink shirt, and a silk tie with a perfect knot, offered his hand. I took it and shook it; he smiled at me with a curious smile. He had blond hair that was turning white and some becoming wrinkles that gave him a look of wisdom. He had small blue eyes that he glared with through his delicate, metal-framed glasses.

"Hello," he said in that deep voice of his.

As I understood that, I responded in English. "Hello, my name is Abbas Kazerooni."

The man chuckled at me and then turned to the other man that had entered the room before me and spoke. I could not understand what he said, but they both laughed. The Persian-looking man also came up to me and shook my hand.

"Hello, Abbas," he said in Farsi. "I am a translator. They were expecting you, and they asked me to come in and help you."

'Thank you," I said in English.

I was still standing and completely awed by this magnificent office. There were old-school pictures on the walls and more oil paintings and souvenirs from all over the world. There were pictures of the man in the beige suit with Margaret Thatcher. I knew who she was because my father always used to talk about her. On his mahogany desk laid fancy fountain pens and beautifully framed pictures of what must have been the man's family.

The man in the suit gestured for me to sit down. Again, in my limited English I spoke. "Thank you."

The man smiled and then turned his head toward some papers. I recognized some of them as the documents that I had given my spectacled friend ten days previously. He then turned his head toward the translator and spoke very quickly and firmly for a few minutes. The translator made a few notes, and then he turned his toward me and began to speak.

"This, Abbas," he said, "is the man in charge of the consulate. He is a very important man."

"I can tell."

"He does not usually get personally involved in cases, but on hearing about your story, he decided to look for himself."

"Thank you," I said, again in English. This was making the man laugh. It appeared to be the center of a ten-word, English vocabulary.

"He says that it is important that you do not lie about anything, because that would mean that you will never get a visa for England."

"I know. I told the other man only the truth." I told him firmly.

The translator spoke to the man, and they exchanged a few more sentences before he turned to me again. As he was about to speak, a lady knocked on a side door to the office and walked in without a response from the man. She had a tray inn her hands. On it was a cup of hot chocolate, in a delicate china cup, and some biscuits. In addition, there was a glass of water. She gave the water to the translator and then laid down the rest in front of me. I was really taken aback and was not sure that they were for me. I did not touch anything until the translator was instructed to tell me something.

"The councilor says that it is all for you," he said smiling. "He said it is his son's favorite."

With that, the councilor picked up one of the frames and showed me a picture of his son with his wife. Hesitantly, I picked up the cups, making sure I did not spill anything, and I sipped it. The taste of that chocolate is still fresh in my mind. It was so delicious, and I think I downed the rest of it in a few gulps. The translator got us back on track by continuing.

"The councilor says that he knows that you have told the truth so far, as your story has been verified by their checks. He just wants you to be warned in case you think about lying in the future. He is just trying to help you."

"Okay."

"He says that he just wanted to meet you, and he is pleased that he has. He says that he likes you."

"Thank you," again I spoke in English at the councilor. He nodded at me.

The translator continued, "He says that he sympathizes with your situation and wants to help you, but he cannot guarantee anything."

"Thank you."

"Do you have any questions?"

I thought about it before answering him. "Yes, I just wanted to know how long these things take?"

The men conferred for a few minutes before the translator began to talk to me again. "The councilor says that there is no guideline for these things, and he cannot give you a specific time scale, because he does not want to disappoint you. However, he does say that he has a boy very similar in age to you, and he knows that he does not want him to be alone in Istanbul. He says that he will really try his best for you, but again, he wants you to know that there are no guarantees. After a certain point, it goes out of his hands."

"Thank you very much," I said to the man.

"Very much," he said with an ironic tone. He smiled though, and through his eyes, I could tell that he genuinely did like me.

"So what should I do now?" I asked.

"You have to go away now and come back in six weeks," he said.

"Six weeks?"

"Yes, I'm afraid so," he said. "This is the date you should come back.'

He handed me a piece of paper with a date and a time written on it.

"I will be here again to translate for you," he continued. "They have the hotel details in case they need to get in touch with you before that."

"Thank you."

The men both stood up, and I immediately followed suit. The councilor walked up to me and shook my hand again and said something to the translator to interpret for me.

"The councilor says look after yourself, and he hopes to see you soon."

"Thank you."

With that, councilor accompanied me to the door where a lady was waiting to take me back to the main consulate area. As I left the room, I took one more look at what I later discovered was a room that epitomized quintessential Englishness!

As I left the consulate, I did not know whether to be happy or sad. I had to wait six weeks, but the most important man in that consulate had taken a liking to me. I stood at the bus stop and waited for the bus. I was very hungry and wanted to get back. It was already getting late, and there was only about one hour of sunlight left. The bus, however, did not appear for about twenty or thirty minutes. In the meantime, I was thinking how my father was going to react when I told him what had taken place. I was thinking that he might order me to return to Iran and try and save the rest of his money. These thoughts once again caused me great stress, and I found it very difficult to cope. I was getting better at it, but it was difficult not to stress internally about the different scenarios that every situation brought.

The bus did eventually did come, and by the time it dropped me off by the marker, it was almost dark. Luckily, the main road was lit, but the road that the hotel was situated on was not. I made my way down the main road and then turned onto my own street. I had never walked in the dark before, and it scared me. The street was not incredibly busy, but as it was the main-road side of the hotel, a few people would come and go. From my room, I would have complained that I could hear all the noises from the street, but when I walked down that street, it seemed terribly silent. The only lights that cleared my way for me were from the houses and flats. I could see my hotel and decided to run the rest of the journey, as I was too nervous. I managed to make my way to the lobby and landed on the lobby steps panting. To my great surprise, I saw Mourat taking my place behind the box cleaning some shoes. It looked really funny, because the stools were not designed for adults, and he was too big for it. I laughed at him as I walked through the door.

"What are you laughing at?" he asked smiling.

"Nothing!" I replied as I walked past him.

"Oi, where are you going?" he asked. "Don't you want to carry on for me?"

"No, I have to go and get some food first. I am really hungry."

"What about when I get hungry?" he said sarcastically. "Do you see me go and get food?"

"Yeah," I said as I darted out of the lobby. I went up to my room and got into some more comfortable clothes. I checked that my money was still there, and it was. I took only a few hundred Liras with me and returned downstairs. As I did, I saw Mourat shaking his hands as if he had just cleaned them while walking out of the kitchen. Suddenly, he burst out laughing at me.

"What?" I asked.

"Your jeans." I looked down at them and noticed that they looked a little stripy.

"I don't understand."

"You are not the first," he said knowingly, "and you certainly won't be the last."

"What?"

"When you cleaned your clothes, you didn't rub them together hard enough. That means that the lighter parts are cleaner than the darker parts."

"Oh," I said. I felt a little stupid, but it did not bother me that much. I was more interested in the food.

I had just walked out of the lobby when Mourat chased me outside. "Phone call, Abbas," he screamed after me.

"Already?" I asked as I ran to the booth. I picked up the phone. "Hello?"

"Abbas," my father said cheerfully, "how did it go?"

"Hi, Baba," I said. "Oh, well, it went okay I think."

"What happened?"

"Well, I met with the guy in charge of the consulate."

"The ambassador?"

"I think so," I said. "The guy called him something else, but he does not usually get involved in these kinds of cases."

"So why did you meet?"

"Because he wanted to meet me for himself, and he likes me. He said that he will try and help me if he can."

"That is great news."

"But he said that there are no guarantees," I explained, "and that I have to go back in six weeks."

"Six weeks?"

"He said it takes time," I said, "but if they get any news, they will call me at the hotel."

"So what are you going to do for six weeks alone?"

"I've been here almost a month, Baba," I said. "I'll be okay. Besides the man said that he has a son my age, and he doesn't like seeing me here alone, and he will try his best for me."

"He said that?"

"Yes."

"How did you speak to him?"

"He had got a real translator."

"Wow, they got a translator for you! That is good news."

"So I will just sit here and wait."

"We'll see."

I did not know what he meant by that, but I was almost hoping he would tell me to go back.

"Is Maman there?"

"Yeah, hold on." That really took me by surprise.

"Hello, my darling. How are you?"

"I'm good, Maman," I said, all cheered up. "How are you?"

"Missing my baby."

"Maman!" I said almost blushing.

"My man, sorry," she corrected herself.

"Yeah, I went to the consulate and saw the most important man there. He said he will try and help me."

"I hear, Sweetness," she said with such great affection. "Well done! I'm so proud of you." I could have almost scripted exactly what I wanted her to say to me. However, she said it by herself. I guess she knew her son. She was saying all the things that I wanted to hear, and it was so pleasing and encouraging when she said them.

"Thank you, Maman."

"So, Abbas," she asked, "what do you do with your time when you are not at the consulate?" I was not sure if she had guessed that I was up to something.

"I watch a lot of television and play backgammon."

"You do, huh?"

"Yeah."

"Well, you take care of yourself, Abbas," she said firmly. "Don't you get into any trouble, because you have a lot of time on your hands now."

"I won't, Maman. I'll be careful."

"Good boy," she said, "I know you will."

"Well, you guys better go. The bill will get big."

"We'll ring again soon," she said, "you look after yourself, my darling." I did not cry after that conversation, but the concept of six more weeks alone was not something that I wanted to consider.

When I came out of the booth, I saw that Mourat was not at reception. I presumed that he was in the kitchen or in the television lounge. I did not really want to leave the hotel, but it had been over twenty-four hours since I last had a meal. I knew that the corner shop was not too far, and so I decided to walk as briskly as I could. The street was like a ghost town. Once again, I could not hear any noises. The only noise that I could hear was the wind channeling along the street. The atmosphere felt ominous, and deep down I felt something was wrong. Before I knew it, I was more than halfway to the shop, and I thought that I should carry on with my journey. My heart rate was already up, and I was really nervous. I still had not seen anyone since leaving the hotel. The only thing that I could see plainly was the lights of the corner shop.

Suddenly, from nowhere, an arm reached out and held me by the neck and pulled me into a thin, dark alleyway. I was absolutely terrified. A thin, sharp-looking man smacked my head against the wall in the alley and put a knife to my throat. He had heavy stubble and small eyes. That is all I seem to remember about the way he looked. He had a heavy cloak or a blanket over his shoulder. The one thing that sticks in my memory was that he stank of alcohol. His breath was pungent, and the way he breathed on me at close proximity made me physically sick. He was at first whispering something at me in Turkish. I did not really understand him, but he kept showing me a small bag with something in it.

"I'm sorry," I whispered, "this is all I have." I opened up my hands to reveal around 250 Liras, which was nothing. Either the fact that I did not understand him or the fact that I did not have money angered him. So his voice began to get a little louder. I kept repeating "This is all I have" in Farsi, but he seemed to get more and more aggravated. Still holding the knife to my throat, he began to search my pockets. Of course, he found nothing in them, and then he began to get even more frustrated.

He picked me up and threw me against the opposite wall of the alley. My head was hurting quite badly from the second bang. He followed me and held me by the neck and pressed in the knife hard against the skin of my throat. I was shaking and had given up speaking. I looked at the man's eyes, and he merely punched me across my cheekbones. It hurt me, but not as much as I expected it to have done. He was drunk and was not in complete control.

I was sure that my time had come, and that I was going to die. I closed my eyes and I felt the knife blade going a little deeper. This was it for sure; it had all happened so quickly, and all I was thinking about was dying where my parents could not find me. In that flash second, my mother and father were what came into my mind. My eyes were still closed, when out of nowhere, my name echoed down the alley.

"Abbas? Abbas? Abbas?"

I was sure I was imagining it, but I opened up my eyes in hope anyway. It was Mourat. For a few seconds, my attacker stood up and stared at Mourat, who stood his ground. Then the attacker turned around and ran down the alley. Immediately, I got up and pretended I was okay. My heart was racing at a thousand miles an hour. I walked onto the street and Mourat lay a hand on my shoulder and then onto my neck. I also touched it and saw that blood was dripping from it. It was not a serious cut, but it was deep enough to cause bad bleeding. I suddenly realized that my head was hurting, and I also touched that. I saw that the back of my head was also bleeding. Again, it was not really serious, but blood was certainly present. As I touched my head, I realized that tears were streaming down my cheeks.

"Are you okay?" Mourat asked.

I could only nod, as I knew that if I spoke I would have become hysterical. The control of my emotions at that point was something that really surprised me. Then I noticed Mourat staring at my jeans again. He surely could not be staring at the stripes at a time like this I thought. I looked anyway, only to realize that I had wet myself. I looked in the alley, and there was a pool of urine covering where I had been pinned. This made me sob a little more. This was the only time Mourat saw me cry, but he also witnessed me wet myself. I could not look at him. I felt extremely low and humiliated. I had really thought that I was going to die. This was my lowest point in Istanbul by a distant mile, and Mourat was a true gentleman.

"It's okay, Little Man," he said softly. "Tell me what you wanted from the shop and I will get it for you." I shook my head to indicate nothing.

"It's okay. You go back. I'll watch you into the hotel," he said. "I know what you eat; I'll get it for you."

I nodded again to say thank you. As I turned around, he called me again. "Little Man?"

"Yeah?" I sobbed as I turned around.

"It's okay. No one will know about this unless you want them to."

"Thank you."

He stood perfectly still and watched me walk all the way back to the hotel and returned to the shop for me once I was safe. I had experienced humanity at the extreme ends of the spectrum of good and evil within such a short space of time. However, I was in no state to appreciate the ironies of humanity at that particular time and space.

As soon as I approached the lobby, I checked that there was no one there and then ran up the stairs to my room. I did not want anyone else to see me in that state. I walked into my room and locked it behind me and went straight into the bathroom. I was now crying freely. I could not believe how close I had come to death. I just wanted to be home now. I really thought about ringing my father. I wanted to give this up. This was a stupid idea, and my father should have known better than to send me to a city like Istanbul all alone. I cried while I took off my clothes, wetting my wounds. My neck was bleeding a lot worse than my head, even though my head was hurting more. I stood in the shower and stared at myself in the mirror. My face was blown up to on the left-hand side. What *have I done so bad that I deserved this?* I kept thinking to myself. After my shower, I had decided to go and ring home. I was sure that this was the final straw. I had really tried my hardest, but it just wasn't good enough.

In reflection, I think God must have been watching me that night because Mourat never left the hotel on his shift. He had ran out of cigarettes, and he did not have anyone to send for him. So he had gone while I had been on the telephone. On his way back, he had witnessed my attack and disturbed the attacker. That was the only time that I ever witnessed Mourat leave the hotel on his shift. I am sure that there was some kind of divine intervention on that night.

When I was out of the shower, I sat in my pajamas on the side of my bed, not knowing what to do. The bleeding had kind of stopped on my neck, and my head was just hurting. Suddenly, there was a knock at the door.

I did not respond until Mourat called out, "Abbas, it's me Mourat." I opened the door and let him in without showing myself to the outside.

"Here," he said, "I've got some bread, cheese, yogurt, water, coke, and some chocolate for you."

"I did not want to argue with him over what I wanted or didn't want, and so I reached for my money on the bedside cabinet.

"Don't be silly;" he said softly, "it's on me."

"No," I said, "take it."

"Don't make me throw you out of my hotel," he said with a smile.

"Thank you," I said, "for everything."

"I didn't do anything," he said. "Oh here, this is for you too." He had some ice. "Put it on your head and face."

"Okay."

"Do you need to see a doctor?"

"No," I said firmly.

"Okay," he said, "do you need anything else?"

"No, thank you."

"That's no problem, Little Man," he said. "You rest well, and if you want anything, just let me know okay?"

"Okay."

Mourat then left the room and I was alone once again. I locked the door and stared at the food. I only wanted water. I could not each anything else. I wished that the incident with the man slapping me on the main had taken place again instead of that night's events. Before I had thought it could not have gotten any worse, but it had. I sat on the bed crying for what seemed like hours. I eventually found myself half-asleep on the floor. So I got up and got into bed. I thought how glad I was that my parents had not called after that incident, because I would not have controlled myself. Once in bed, I had changed my mind and decided that I was not going to tell my parents because I know that they would have blamed themselves. However, I craved for my mother to hold me that night. I needed her more than ever, and I could not even speak to her. I felt so alone and sad. I had no more emotions left inside of me. I just did not know what to do with myself. Eventually, I fell as asleep as ever with the lights on and with the pictures of my family.

I woke up the next morning around 4 a.m. I had a nightmare about the previous night, and my head was still spinning and hurting like before. I reached for the water on the bedside cabinet, when I realized that my sheets were wet. I had wet myself again. I started to cry and so desperately wanted to call Iran, but I could not bring myself to. I needed someone to help me and be there for me; most of all, I needed my mother. I could not bear to see anyone. I took off my sheets and washed them in the shower, half-heartedly. My head was hurting so much, and the last thing that I wanted to do was wash my sheets. I did not want anyone to know that I had wet myself so I had to do it. After that, I had shower and returned to bed. I tried sleeping on the dry parts of the bed but it was not really working, and the mattress was too heavy to roll over. I lay there still crying and drifted in and out of sleep.

The next day I did not get up out of bd. When the cleaner knocked on the door, I did not let her come in. I stayed in bed and stared at the wall. I did not want to speak to anyone and had no energy for work. My head was still hurting, and I needed rest. I think I was very depressed, and I felt like I could not do anything. All I wanted to do was to cry and to sleep. Mourat did come to my door and spoke to me through the door, but I just told him that I needed rest. He was understanding about it and left me to my own devices. I was just dreading my parents calling me, because I did not know if I could hide this from my mother. I wanted to be with her so much, but I did not want her to go through the inevitable guilt trip that would ensue if I told them of the previous night's events. By the end of that day, I did eat a little bread, which made feel a little better, but I was not eating as much as I should have.

For three and a half days, I stayed in my room away from the outside world. I think the only reason that I decided to leave was because I thought I would run out of money and needed to be making money. My thinking was that I did not want my parents to find out about what had taken place, and that would only be achieved if I had money to live on. The swelling had gone down a little on my face, and my head was not pounding as much as it was. I felt very tired, though, probably because I had overslept. Emotionally, I was still down and I went to sleep on the third night, promising myself that I would go downstairs the following morning.

CHAPTER 14

The following morning I rose again, finding I had wet myself. With great difficulty, I forced myself to get up and took my sheets into the shower and attempted to wash them again. The room was getting very stuffy and the moisture was at its all time low. It was early morning, and so I edged my way past the curtains and opened the window for the first time since I had been there. With a rustic creak, the window edged itself open for a fresh breeze to come through. It was a cold breeze, but I did not mind it. I sat on the edge of my bed and watched the remainder of the sun make its way above the Istanbul horizon. In my mind, I was going downstairs, but it was still a huge move for me. I can remember waiting for the sun to make its way above the buildings opposite. It was such a calm morning; I was shutting out all the noises from the street below. Such solitude only makes one think, and at such a tender age, I am not sure it is a very healthy factor.

Slowly, I put on my clothes and walked out of my room. I locked the door behind me and started to walk downstairs. I was dreading seeing Mourat. I was still humiliated and felt embarrassed about seeing him. I knew, however, that I had to see him at some point. I walked into a deserted lobby with Mourat in a deep sleep on his desk. It was still very early. So I decided to go into the kitchen, got myself a glass of tea, and retired in the television lounge. There were a lot of empty glasses and ashtrays from the previous night, which still needed to be cleaned. This was not really my job, because I was only working for tips, but I knew that if I settled in front of the television I might not get up again. I was so tired, even though I had been in bed for three days. I guess it was a case of oversleeping.

I set to work cleaning, when I heard Mourat walk in. "You know you won't get paid any extra for that?" he said jokingly.

I smiled at him. "I know, but I needed something to do."

"Why don't you write a letter home?" he asked.

It was a good question, but I was not sure that I could cope with writing home and not saying anything about what had happened. Mourat was being great about the whole situation. He made it easy for me, because he did not talk about that night at all. He was being as normal as he possibly could. Perhaps he thought that if I wanted to talk to him about it, then I would do just that. This, of course, I never did.

"Maybe I should write a letter home," I said. "It has been a while."

"Good," he simply said with a thoughtful smile on his face, "besides I have a match for you today. You better get practicing."

"So should he," I said, trying to make the atmosphere a little lighter.

"I hope not!"

I began to walk back toward the reception and then stopped to ask, "Is the paper and the envelope . . . ?"

"Where it always is," he interrupted. I smiled and began to walk off, when I stopped again and looked at Mourat.

"Mourat?"

"Yes?"

"Can I ask for a favor?" I asked pathetically.

"As long as it has nothing to do with money!" he replied.

"It doesn't!" I said laughing. He always had the ability to make me smile. Thinking back to that time, he had great patience with me for a man who did not have children.

"Well, what is it?"

"Can you please ask the cleaner not to clean my room until tomorrow?" I asked. I felt that maybe I should come up with a story to explain the request, because I thought that he was going to ask me. "It's just that the all my clothes are . . ."

"Sure thing," he replied. He did not ask any questions, and his interruption was solid and to the point. The more I got to know Mourat, the more I realized that deep down he was a good man. With the sheets off my mind, I returned to the lobby. Slowly, I reached for the paper and the envelope and took my usual seat next to the phone booth. I stared at the paper for a long time without writing anything. I did not know what I could say had happened since we last spoke. It was a hard thing to do, but I thought I should write a letter, because when my parents did eventually call, I would need to say something. So the letter could act as a dress rehearsal. With careful consideration, I put pen to paper:

Dear Maman,

I hope you are well. I am doing okay. It has been pretty boring since my consulate visit. Nothing has really happened. I have watched a lot of television and slept a lot. It was so good to speak to you though, Maman. I had really missed you. I wish you could have been here with me. Maybe while I am killing time to go to the consulate again, you can sort out your papers and join me. It would be so good if you came here. I could show you everything and show you how everything works. I know before I left I never used to tell you how much I love you, but if I saw you again, I would not be embarrassed, even if my friends were there!

So how is Mamanjoon? Is she still up to her old tricks? Tell her I miss her too. Tell her now that I am eight. I am a real man!

Well, I better go now. I hope you can come here soon.

I love you,

Your son,

Abbas

As I wrote that letter, I really wanted to cry and write the truth, but I had promised myself that I would keep the attack a secret. I did not cry because Mourat had reentered the lobby, and I did not want him to see me crying again. With internal anguish, I sealed the envelope and addressed it so that it could be posted. People then began to come down stairs, one by one. Even though the hotel did not offer breakfast, a lot of the Persians required tea before their day. Therefore, I put myself back to work with great urgency and efficiency in order to take my mind off things. I was also soliciting my shoe cleaning with every glass of tea that I served. The work did make me feel a little better, but the physical scars were still there. They were my reminders of that incident for two weeks until they fully healed. My head was still scabbing, but because of my hair, it was difficult to see it. The most obvious scar was the bruise on my face though. People would always look at it, but hardly ever dared to say anything. Some people asked and I used to tell them that I got into a fight with some local boys. There was also the scar on my neck from the point of the knife.

After the events of that tragic evening, I had decided that I would confine myself to the hotel even more than before. This, therefore, meant that I could no longer do the package runs for Hector, even though the money was so good. I was only going to leave the hotel to swap money, to go to the consulate, and to get food, all way before the sun would go down. I actually did need some Liras, and I needed food that day that I reemerged from my room. Therefore, after I had completed my letter, I decided I should go to town while it was morning. I really did not want to leave the hotel, but I had to. I had not eaten for two days, and my Liras had gone toward the hotel bill. I had not made any money for three days either.

I did not want Mourat to see me leave the hotel, as I thought that he would ask me if I was going to be all right or something on those lines. I did not want any fuss, and so I waited for him to leave the reception area for a brief moment, and I was out of the door. I was doing a very basic thing by walking down the street, but to me at that particular moment, it was a huge event. My heart was racing, and I was aware of everyone around me. I thought that I had maybe got a little relaxed with my surroundings, and that is why I was attacked. My state of paranoia was at an all-time high. I walked briskly down the road with my hands in my pockets, grabbing the $60 I had in my pocket with dear life. I had fifty that I wanted to change and a marked ten that I had to exchange with Hector. I was not really thinking, because that $10 was still good. It just had some writing in the corner. Nobody would have minded that, but I just wanted to finish things properly.

I eventually got the market place, and I headed straight for Hector's shop. I opened the door to see Hector sitting on a chair behind the counter examining some piece of jewelry. He looked up and saw me. He was initially smiling, but upon seeing my face he stopped his grin and suddenly became very serious.

"What happened to you, my friend?"

"Nothing," I said, "it was nothing."

"It obviously was," he said with a firm voice. "Who did this to you?"

I looked at him with a little fear, because Hector was gradually getting angry. I did not say anything.

"Who did this to you, Abbas," he asked louder.

"I don't know."

"Don't you protect anyone," he ordered me. "Whomever it was will regret this. I'll take care of it, Abbas. Just tell me who did it to you."

"I don't know," I said softly. "I promise."

"What happened?"

"I was going to a shop to buy some food near where I live, and some guy attacked me and took me into a dark alley."

"Why?"

"I don't know," I said. "I had never seen him before, and he grabbed me from the alley where I couldn't see him. I was lucky, because the hotel manager walked past and scared him away."

Hector looked into my eyes really hard. I was absolutely terrified. I had never seen him like this before. I thought he was going to kill me, never mind this man.

"What did he look like?" he asked.

"I can't really remember. It was dark and I was scared."

"I know, but do you remember anything?"

"Yeah, he had heavy stubble, and he was your height, and he smelled really bad."

"What else?"

"He had small eyes and looked really rough. Oh, and he was very thin."

"I'm not sure what I can do with that, but if you ever see this guy again, you come straight here and tell me. Okay?"

"Okay."

There was a brief silence as we both got our breath. I did not know what Hector would have done if he found that man, but honestly I did not care. That man deserved everything he got.

"So will you have a drink, Abbas?" he asked in a more relaxed tone.

"No, thank you," I said. "I just want to change my money, and . . ." I paused there.

"And what?"

"And . . . well, I wanted to swap my last, marked $10 bill, because I do not want to take the packages anymore."

"I see," he said. "Why?"

"I just don't, and it has nothing to do this," I said pointing to my face.

"Okay."

"Sorry."

"Okay," he replied, "if that is what you want, then no problem."
It was going a little easier than I had imagined.

"Thank you," I said as I handed him the $60.

"But will you do me a favor?"

"Sure," I said.

"Will you do one more drop today, and that will be the last one."
I stared at him as if to say no, but I could not bring myself to say that.

"It's okay, Abbas. I understand."

I was being very reasonable, but I was not sure if he expected
me to agree to this last drop because he was being so nice about it. I just
kept my mouth shut.

"You better come back here and swap money though," he
joked.

"I will."

"Good, and if you see that guy again, you come straight here,
and I will take care of everything for you."

"Thank you."

"No problem," he said as he counted out my money. He then
handed me a bundle of Liras, and a new $10 note.

"Actually, will you please swap the ten too?" I asked.

"Sure."

He handed me all the money, and I left. I was not sure if I should
return to him in the future, but it would have been difficult if he had seen
me in another shop. He had been more than fair with me in all of our
previous transactions.

I made my way back to the hotel, but the return journey did not
feel so bad. I was in deep thought about what had happened in Hector's
shop. I was wondering why he was so concerned for me and why he
wanted to take care of things. His behavior had scared me a little. I got
to the hotel and decided to keep walking to the shop. It felt very strange
walking down the same path again. There were plenty of people; I did
not feel afraid, but I knew that I would not like walking past the alleyway. When I did, I wanted to look down it, but I was too frightened. I
closed my eyes and walked briskly until I had walked past the spot of
the attack. I reached the shop and began to pick up the usual things when
I noticed the shopkeeper looking at my face. He was serving someone
else, but he was looking at me. I pretended that I did not notice and

carried on with my business. When I went to pay, he just looked at me and did not say anything. I did not like the way that he was looking at me. It was a look of distrust. He must have thought that I had been up to no good. I thought that he was a kind man, but he was different on this occasion. I did not understand why people were so willing to be rude to you when you had been nothing short of polite to them. It made absolutely no sense to me.

When I returned, Hector was not in the lobby. I took up my things to my room and had a small meal. It was the first time I had eaten properly since that night. Once again, it was a lonely feeling eating by myself. I was getting sick and tired of bread, cheese, and yogurt. It was the cheapest option for me. Vegetables had been missing from my diet for some time now, but it made no difference to me. I was too young to even think about such things. I just knew that I had to eat cheap food that would fill me up. I chewed silently on the bread as I stared at the photographs. Knowing my mother the way that I did, I knew that she would not cope seeing me in that state. They were due to call me soon, and I knew that I had to control myself, especially with my mother. She always brought out the more emotional side of me. I was now beyond crying. I had no more energy to cry. For three days, I had hibernated inside of my room, and if I was not sleeping, then I had been thinking and crying. I was trying my hardest to overcome this event, but I needed more support than was available to me.

I returned downstairs to find Mourat dosing in the television lounge. I took the initiative and made him a glass of tea and left it in front of him in case he woke up. I spent the rest of the time between the shoe cleaning box and the bar. It appeared that the guests had missed me. That cheered me up a little, and it was nice to be appreciated, even by strangers. At around eight o'clock, there was a dip in business, and I took it upon myself to take a break in front of the television. Knight Rider had just started when Mourat rushed into the lounge.

"Abbas?"

I looked round to see him. "Yes?"

"Phone call."

Without hesitation I rushed through to the lobby and into my phone booth. I shut the door behind me, and I took a deep breath. I picked up the receiver and took one more deliberate pause before speaking. "Hello?"

"Abbas, my darling?" my mother voice echoed. It was so good to hear her loving voice again.

"Maman," I screamed, "how are you?"

"I'm good, Sweetness," she said, "and how are you?"

"I'm okay—no, I'm good," I forced out.

"What are you doing?" she asked gently.

"Watching television," I said more cheerfully. "Knight Rider is on. It is a great show."

"Good."

"Where is Baba?" I asked.

"Not in at the moment," she said softly. "I just thought that I would call and see how you are."

"Thank you, Maman."

"My darling, it's my pleasure," she said affectionately. "I wanted to hear your voice. I miss you."

"I miss you too, Maman," I said more emotionally.

"Are you really okay, my baby?"

"Yes, why?"

"I don't know," she said. "It's just something."

I knew that she felt something was wrong, but luckily, she did not know exactly what.

"No, I'm fine, Maman."

"Promise me."

"I promise." I could not believe that I had promised that I was telling the truth to her when I was not. It was very difficult for me to lie to my mother, and if she had seen my face, she would have known differently. I am not just talking about the scars; I am talking about the expressions that she knew all too well. As I promised her, I remember trying to justify that lie to myself. I thought that technically I was okay, so in that respect I was not lying. Also, if it was a lie, I was only doing it to not hurt her more than she already was.

"Well, if you promise me," she said, "I believe you."

"Have you got any more letters, Maman?" I asked trying to change the subject a little.

"Yes, my darling," she said. "I love them."

"Oh good," I said smiling, "I was just wondering, that's all."

214

"No, they are all here, Abbas," she told me. "I read them all the time." As she said it, I smiled to myself thinking how many times I had read her letter to me.

"How is Mamanjoon?"

"Good," she said, "she sends her love."

"Maman, you better go," I told her. "Your bill's going to be huge."

"Are you sure?"

"Yeah."

Of course, deep down, I did not want her to leave, but I knew their situation. My guess was that my father knew nothing of that call, and it had not been planned. My mother had taken a quick opportunity to call me while my father had gone out. I knew not to say anything in the next conversation with my father. My mother had not asked me to keep it a secret, but I knew parents pretty well.

The conversation with my mother had made me feel a lot better. So with a smile, I returned to Knight Rider and actually managed to forget everything for the remainder of the program. For the rest of the evening, I served drinks and mingled with the guests. The old nickname of Rocky was reemerging, but once again, I did not mind. That night I went to bed feeling tired, which was good, as I hoped that I could get a good night's sleep. As I entered the room, I realized that I had to put my sheets back on my bed, but they were still damp. So I just lay on the bed and stared at the photographs until I fell asleep.

During the next five and a half weeks, I only left the hotel three times a week and only in the mornings for food. I only went to the market place twice, and I exchanged more money so that I did not have to leave the hotel. Hector was still giving me good rates, and he never mentioned the packages again. I made myself a prisoner within the hotel and knew that it was the best thing for me. I very rarely got bored, as I made myself busy with jobs around the hotel. The backgammon games were not so popular anymore, but they did take place once in a while. My main jobs were serving drinks and cleaning shoes.

The phone calls from my parents were getting less frequent and shorter in length. It was obvious that financially they were not doing very well. The longest period between calls was one week. The worst part of that period of time was the fact that I could not sleep very well.

I had begun to wet the bed more and more frequently. I spent hours washing sheets, trying to save face in front of the hotel staff. Many nights I cried myself to sleep again, and my longing for my parents never seemed to disappear. There were no really dramatic events in this time period, which I thanked God for, but sometimes small things would upset me—things like children with their parents or eating alone or sleeping without having anyone to say good night to. Their pictures were all I had. The first four weeks had certainly been harder. Maybe I had got more used to my environment, and I had learned to do just enough without getting into any kind of trouble. The second four or five weeks seemed less dramatic, but it certainly made it easier on me. However, in this period I was still dealing with the trauma caused by the first period. It had created a mental state of paranoia; I had become a recluse inside the hotel and could not sleep very well.

CHAPTER 15

The day of my consulate meeting came a lot slower than I had anticipated. I had thought that if I kept myself busy then the time would go faster. It had gone fast at times, but I had really felt the time. I was always looking at the date and wishing that the day would arrive. This, of course, put pressure on my financial situation too. I was beginning to think that I should ask Hector for a delivery job back, but I really did not want to do it.

When I woke up the morning of my meeting, I was hoping for some type of answer, because I did not know how much longer I was going to be able to cope with staying in that hotel. It was not too bad for a short period, but I had been there over two months now.

I stepped off the bus very casually, but inside my heart was racing. I did not know why, but I thought that something was going to happen that afternoon that would change everything. I walked through the gates, past the guards, and up the drive. I walked through security without too much difficulty and entered the main building. This time, I was not sure whether to reach for the ticket or not, and so I looked over to my spectacled friend who saw me as soon as I stepped inside the building. Once again, he waved at me, and this time I needed no second telling. I walked straight to the side door and waited. Within a few minutes, the man came and opened the door for me. He shook my hand this time, and he seemed even friendlier than before. It was strange, because the first time that I had met this man, he seemed like a robot without feelings. Now he seemed like a good human being. Once again, I was taken to the door that led into the councilor's office. I sat outside expecting to be there for a good hour, when suddenly the door opened. The councilor and the translator were both there. The councilor was wearing a navy suit this time, equally as fetching as his beige one. He guided me in and shook my hands.

"Hello, Abbas."

"Hello."

"Please sit down," he said in English, but I took the hand gesture as my guide, as I did not understand what he was saying.

"Hello again," the translator said in Farsi.

"Hello."

The hot chocolate and the biscuits were already there waiting for me. The councilor pointed to them indicating that I should help myself.

"Thank you," I said in English. Immediately, he started to laugh as my short repertoire of English words had suddenly started again.

"The councilor has updated me on what is going on. So before we start speaking, I am just going to tell you what he told me."

"Okay."

"The situation is very complicated. Your cousin has signed papers to say that he will be your guardian, and that is the most important factor. He has also confirmed that you will be going there to avoid going to war and for your education."

"That is correct," I confirmed.

"So far your story has been completely right on your cousin's occupation and other details that we have asked for."

"Okay."

"That is usually not enough to issue a visa, because everyone would try that approach."

"So what does that mean?" I asked.

"Well, the councilor has suggested that your case be considered much faster than the usual time period because of your situation," he explained. "He has done all the written work, and then he has to write a final report after today's meeting. Then a decision should be made, but once again, he is very adamant that you understand that there are no guarantees."

"I understand."

"Good."

Then the translator began to speak to the councilor again, as my head wondered around the room, looking at the monuments around his grand office again. I did not know if what he was telling me was good or bad. The one thing that I could tell was that hopefully I would get an answer one way or another very soon. The councilor smiled at me as the translator continued.

"The councilor wants to know how you are."

I looked at the councilor in the eyes and said, "Okay."

The councilor looked straight back into my eyes and nodded. He did not say anything for a while and then said something to the translator.

"When did you last speak to your parents?" he asked.

"Four or five days ago," I said, "but they have no money now, because we had to sell everything so that I could come here."

The translator relayed my words, only for another knowing nod from the councilor. Then he asked something as he looked at me.

"The councilor wants to know if there is anything that you want to tell him that may help you."

"I don't know if it will help me," I said, "but ask him to tell me something soon. I am really depressed here, and I don't know how long I can pretend to my parents that I am okay. The last time I was here, as I went back to my hotel, I was hungry. On my way to the shops, I was attacked. I had a bleeding neck, a bleeding head, and a bruised face. You can't see it now, as they have healed, but I have people who saw these scars. Please just tell me if I can go or not, because I can't sleep. I can't leave the hotel without feeling scared for my life, and I miss my parents. If I go back to Iran, I may get sent to the war. I know that my father would hate me for saying this, but at least I would see my parents before they send me. So please, just ask the councilor to tell me soon."

I began crying. I could not believe that I had told them. They were complete strangers, and I told them pretty much everything. I just hoped that it would help solve my case. The translator told the councilor everything. The councilor then stood to his feet, which immediately made me do the same. He then gestured that I sit down. He came close to me and tilted my head. He looked at my neck and placed his index finger exactly where I had been cut. As he did, he talked to the translator.

"He says that you were very lucky."

"I know."

Then the councilor told the man something very quickly, and then the translator also stood up. "The councilor says come back in two weeks, and he will see what he can do for you. He also says continue to stay in your hotel unless you have to get out."

"Thank you." With that the councilor showed me to the door, shook my hand, and tapped me on the shoulder as if to say "hang in there."

I returned to the hotel pretty disappointed. I had not been told either way. The only thing that was good was that in two weeks I was going to be told whether they would give me a visa or not. That made me worry, because if they did not, what would my father think. I would go back with only about $600 and nothing to show for it. His disappointment in me worried me more than not getting the visa. Therefore, I decided not tell my parents that they would give me an answer in two weeks. I just decided to tell them that I would have to return to the consulate in two weeks. I pondered for many hours about my father's reaction if I was refused for a visa. I think I was preparing myself for the worst, even though I did not think that it would have been fair. So for two more weeks, I stayed within the perimeters and safety of the hotel. I talked to my parents twice very briefly, telling them that I had to go back for another interview. I did my jobs, I stayed out of trouble, and yet I still continued to wet the bed, even if less frequently. Those two weeks crept up on me a lot swifter than the previous five, because I was nervous about going back to the consulate. I did not want to go back, because I was scared of the possible result.

When I got off the bus outside the consulate, I felt a cold breeze rush through my long, thick hair. I knew something with significant consequences would happen that day. I had a feeling deep inside me. With the same ritual, I passed the guards and went up the drive and through security, into the main building. I did not even bother going to the ticket machine. I just waited to get my friend's attention at his booth. When he saw me, he waved me over to his booth. At first, I misunderstood and was about to go to the side door, but he waved again to tell me to come and see him. I was so upset when I saw this. I thought that the councilor did not want to give me a visa, and he did not want to tell me,so I was going to be rejected there and then. I wanted to cry so badly, but I managed to control myself.

My spectacled friend smiled and said, "Passport."

Even I understood that, and so I handed it to him. He looked at it, and then he handed me a piece of paper back. He then began to speak to me, but I did not understand. He showed me his watch and indicated two hours. He waved for me to leave with the piece of paper, and then to come back in two hours. I began to back peddle toward the door to make sure that I was doing the right thing. Luckily, as I did, he started to smile and so I left. I walked out of the consulate, but I was frightened to leave the grounds in case they wanted to see my passport when I wanted to come back in. When I reached the gates, I looked at the guards, showed them my paper, and put up two fingers at them, indicating two hours. They smiled and nodded, which made me feel a little easier. It was one thing getting rejected, but another to lose my passport too.

I walked down the road from the consulate, and there was a little park, which seemed empty. It was so beautiful, probably one of the most beautiful parks I have ever seen. It was very small with little benches around a small square. There was an old couple feeding pigeons, and I sat on another bench watching them. The pigeons were eating from their hands, which amazed me. It had been a long time since I had enjoyed such a simple pleasure. I was still wondering what the outcome at the consulate would be that day. How would I go about telling my father that I had been refused? He had been a lot gentler with me on the telephone in recent conversations, but I still did not want to tell him that. Every few minutes, I would look at my Casio watch, and yet time seemed to have stood still. I was nervous and just wanted to know what was going on.

After one and a half hours, I could not wait any longer and decided to return to the consulate and wait in their building. Once I was in the waiting area, I saw that my spectacled friend had seen me. After he finished with his next client, he walked into the back office and reemerged with the councilor. They both smiled at me and called me over. Suddenly, I actually believe that they were going to give me the visa.

My heart was pounding as fast as the night that I had been attacked. I approached the counter and the councilor opened my passport without saying anything, revealing a shiny visa in my passport. I could not believe my eyes. The councilor walked around and opened the side door so that he could give it to me personally. He shook my hand and said, "Good luck."

"Thank you," I said. "Thank you too," I repeated to my spectacled friend. I took my passport and walked out of the building. On the drive, I opened my passport again and looked at it. It looked so beautiful. I went out of the gates and waited by the bus stop. Everything was going so smoothly. Almost as soon I stood by the stop, the bus emerged. As I sat on the bus, I began to cry. I thought about all the things that had happened to me since leaving Iran—the body and the beating on my first night, the man on the street, and the attack. It had all been worth it. I could not wait until that night. I was going to ring my parents as soon as I got back to the hotel. I knew they would not mind that. To that date, that had been the biggest achievement of my life. I felt that all of my hardships had been worth something. All those times when I had questioned my purpose in Istanbul were a distant memory.

I ran all the way from the bus stop back to the hotel. Out of breath, I ran into the lobby to find Mourat.

"Mourat, Mourat," I called.

"What happened?" he asked.

"I got it! I got it!" I screamed.

"What?"

"My visa," I said as I showed it to him. He was delighted for me. He got off his chair and came round to hug me.

"Well done, Little Man. Well done."

"Thank you," I said, "can I call my parents?"

"Sure," he said, "and if you keep it short, it's on me."

"Wow," I said, "thank you."

I wrote the number for him and ran into the phone booth. I waited, and after about thirty seconds my phone rang. I was about to pick up when I took a deep breath before sharing the news. I picked up to hear a ringing tone. After about five rings, my mother picked up.

"Hello?"

"Maman?"

"Abbas, my darling?" she said all surprised. "What happened?"

"Nothing, Maman, nothing," I said trying to calm her down. "I have some news."

"What?"

"I got it! I got the visa."

The loudest cream came down the phone line. I had the biggest grin on my face. My mother was in real shock.

"Oh, my God. That is wonderful."

"Is Baba there?"

"Karim?" she shouted after him. "So they gave it to you

already?"

"Yes, it is in my passport. I'm looking at it."

"I can't believe it, Abbas," she said. "I never thought that would be possible. You don't know how proud of you I am. What you have done is truly amazing."

"Maman," I called out blushing.

"Here is your father," she said.

"Hello?" he said. "What happened?"

"I got the visa today, Baba."

"You're joking."

"No, honestly, I am looking at it right now."

"Abbas, that is amazing news. Well done, my son. You don't know how proud I am."

"You are?"

"Am I? Do you think anyone could have done this?" he asked seriously.

"I don't know," I said.

"Well they couldn't. You should be proud of yourself, Abbas. You're more than a man to me."

Those words were what I had waited over three months for. I was happier to hear that my father was proud of me than the fact that I had a British visa.

"Thank you, Baba."

"Now we have to get you a ticket to London," he said. "How much money do you have left?"

"Over $600."

"This gets better," he said laughing.

"I will get Mehdi to buy your ticket, and then you can pick it up from British Airways in Istanbul. Then, when you get to London, you can give him your dollars."

"Okay."

"I will ring you tonight to tell you where to pick up your ticket."

"Okay, Baba," I said smiling to myself. "You go now, because my bill will get huge."

"Okay, I'll call you later."

I had the biggest smile on my face; life could not have been any better. I walked out of the booth to see Mourat smiling.

"They were happy, huh?"

"Oh, yes," I said, "just a little bit."

"So when are you leaving?"

"I don't know. They are sending me a ticket to British Airways, which I have to pick up."

"Oh, okay."

"Do you know where that is?"

"Yeah, I'll go with you, if you want."

"Yeah, sure."

"And one more request?"

"Yes?"

"Can I take you to the airport?"

"You'd do that?" I asked.

"Of course I would."

"Thank you."

"It's my pleasure," he said. "We'll go in my car."

"You have a car?"

"Yes."

"I have known you for over three months, and I did not know that."

"It's because I am always here." We both laughed.

Sure enough, my father did ring that night, and it was arranged for me to go the following day to pick up the ticket. My flight was in exactly five days. I could not actually believe I was going to England. I came to Istanbul with the purpose of going there, but I never really thought I would achieve that goal. The next five days were spent cleaning all of my clothes and packing. I got my money from Mourat and exchanged the remaining Liras back into dollars. In the evenings, I still worked serving drinks and cleaning shoes when I had to. Those five days seemed to take longer than the thirteen weeks I had already been there. I was excited about seeing this country that my father had built up for me as the greatest country in the world.

The day of my departure finally came, and to his word, Mourat helped with my bags and took me to the airport in his car. On the way, we did not really speak. Neither of us really knew what to say. Honestly, I was going to miss Mourat. He had tried to trick me a few times, but I caught him. However, he had also saved my life and been a good friend. He had more patience with me than anyone I knew in my childhood, outside of my close family. He was indeed a good man.

At the airport, I checked in and a lady was sent to look after me. This made me laugh, because in an airport and on a plane one cannot be safer, and yet I was given a chaperone. This was it for Mourat and me.

"Well, Little Man," he said, "I guess this is it."

"Yeah."

"Who am I going to find to serve tea like you, huh?"

He was getting quite emotional, which surprised me, as I never knew how fond Mourat was of me.

"You'll find someone."

"Not like you," he said, "and who else is there to keep me on the straight and narrow—and those crazy business ideas?"

"Only one!"

"A good one."

"Thanks," I said embarrassed.

"I'll miss you, Little Man. People like you don't come around too often."

"Thank you, Mourat. I will miss you too."

"I think the lady is waiting, but you take care of yourself, Little Man."

"You too, Mourat. You take care too."

With that, he turned around and disappeared in the crowd. This is where I met my first friend in Istanbul. Without Ahmed's help, I might not have lasted one night in that city. Here was the place again where I lost touch with another friend. That was the last time I ever saw Mourat, but I did think of him from time to time. That was the end of my adventures in Istanbul. The British Airways lady took me straight to the plane where I sat and smiled, looking forward to my future. I imagined that once I was in England everything would be a bed of roses once again. I could not have been more wrong.

I wished I had the wisdom of Winston Churchill when he said, "Now is not the end. It is not even the beginning of the end. But it is perhaps, the end of the beginning."

That quotation could not have summed up the hardships of my life any better. I, however, did not know that.

Contact author Abbas Kazerooni
or order more copies of this book at

TATE PUBLISHING, LLC

127 East Trade Center Terrace
Mustang, Oklahoma 73064

(888) 361 - 9473

Tate Publishing, LLC

www.tatepublishing.com